# Protecting Children: Messages from Europe

## Rachael Hetherington, Andrew Cooper, Philip Smith and Gerti Wilford

Russell House Publishing Ltd

*First published in 1997 by*

Russell House Publishing Limited
38 Silver Street
Lyme Regis
Dorset
DT7 3HS

© Rachael Hetherington, Andrew Cooper, Philip Smith and Gerti Wilford

**British Library Cataloguing-in-Publication Data:**
A catalogue record for this book is available from the British Library.

Hardback ISBN: 1-898924-12-0
Paperback ISBN: 1-898924-11-2

*Typeset by:* Ed Skelly, Berwick upon Tweed

*Printed by:* Bourne Press, Bournemouth

# Contents

# Acknowledgements

We would like to thank all the social workers and academic colleagues who made this book possible. This research on European child protection and child welfare systems started in France, but when we came to extend the work to other countries in Europe, we continued to have good fortune in finding colleagues with whom we were able to develop the same style of co-operative and reflective research that we had practised in France. We would like to thank Rina Gjisen, An Sprangers and Christian Van Uffell from the Sociale Hogeschool and the Institut Superieur de Formation Sociale et de Communication in Brussels, Véronique Freund and Alain Grevot and the Association Jeunesse Culture Loisirs Techniques (JCLT), in Beauvais, Professor Rolf Piquardt from the Fachhochschule in Koblenz, Michael Wohlschlegel from the Jugendamt in Bad Doberan, Dr Edda Samory from the Centro Studi di Servizio Sociale in Bologna, Drs Robert Ploem from the Hogeschoole van Amsterdam, Roisin McGoldrick from the University of Strathclyde in Glasgow and David Crimmens from the University of Humberside in Hull. We are deeply appreciative of the time and energy they have put into this research and of the spirit of inquiry that led them to embark on an unusual project with relatively untested methodology set up by researchers they knew nothing of. Their help and enthusiasm has been crucial.

We are also extremely grateful to the practitioners in all the countries we visited and in this country, who have given up time and shown enthusiasm and commitment to something which was outside their day to day concerns and the many calls on their time. We would particularly like to thank Claude Esposito, Geneviève Huon, Bernd Patczowsky, Liesbet Smeyers and Ursula Wagner, who helped us by providing additional case material and expert opinion.

Angela Spriggs was a member of the research team for the first half of the project, and played a major part in enabling the project to achieve its primary task. We are very grateful for the enthusiasm and initiative that she brought to the research. We are also grateful to Karen Baistow for her help in the final stages.

We have been encouraged throughout by the interest shown in our work by our colleagues in the Department of Social Work at Brunel University College. None of this could have been achieved without the support of the Research Sub-Committee of Brunel University College.

# Foreword
by Rupert Hughes

I am pleased to write an introduction to this book which reports on the research developed by the team which produced 'Positive Child Protection – A view from abroad' about the English and French child protection systems and is now looking comparatively at the systems of seven countries. Countries differ widely in their social, cultural and legal situations and values and at first sight it might seem too difficult to undertake anything other than the most superficial comparison of the societies and particularly of something like the child protection system which I think is greatly affected by these variables. However this book shows that this is mistaken and that it is possible to draw insights out of other systems with which to compare one's own. This is not to say that one can necessarily transfer elements of one system into another but rather, as the authors themselves emphasise, that it is very helpful in striving to improve one's system to look at it from the entirely new perspective of one which is different.

The authors themselves would not claim that the social workers were wholly representative of their countries although they did try to find staff who were typical. This is important when one looks at the response to the given case by the English teams (of which there were several) to a situation in which the family were not co-operating. The Children Act 1989 provided for this with the Child Assessment Order for cases of 'nagging' concern and the frustrated access ground for the Emergency Protection Order for cases of immediate concern. Given the number of child protection enquiries which show that children who should have been seen quickly were not, it is worrying that this was not understood.

The book is strictly about social work in a situation which calls out for interdisciplinary working. To me it reveals that in most countries this is as yet imperfectly understood and accepted.

The most important message I find is the need (but only when there is enough time and some reasonable prospect) for social workers to look for ways of reaching an agreed plan for the child before the potentially traumatic and expensive court process. The continental systems provide this 'space' as the book shows in various ways. Sometimes this is part of an inquisitorial court process itself and the court has the additional function of supervising the case. But although it is becoming more proactive, the English care court is essentially adversarial and is unlikely to give the scope for negotiation which may be needed for agreement on the plan or to be in a position to provide any necessary follow-up. Within the English system however it ought to be possible to supply the 'authority' in other ways.

This comparative work is long overdue. I hope it will not only provide insights for people looking at their own systems but will inspire other researchers to undertake this type of study.

**Rupert Hughes C.B.E.**

# Introduction

This book expands on the research into European child welfare and protection systems begun in *Positive Child Protection: A View from Abroad* (Cooper *et al.*, 1995). In attempting to distil into a book the material from a lengthy and complex research process crossing six national boundaries, we were faced with major problems of selection and organisation. Any of the eight systems we studied would merit a book in its own right, and yet it is the bringing together of the information about all eight systems in one place that is important for us. Below we offer a brief outline of the contents with the intention of giving the reader a map of the strange terrain which she or he is about to explore.

In Section One we are looking at elements of the context of the research from which this book originated. Chapter 1 articulates a vision of the relationship between cross-national research, policy change and practice endeavour. Chapter 2 examines the relationship between child protection and the way that society conceives itself. By way of illustration, the functioning of one particular continental system is explored and compared with that of the English system.

Section Two looks at the research process and findings. In Chapter 3 the complex methodology of the research is described and analysed. Chapter 4 gives a description of the eight different systems of child welfare and child protection that we studied. Chapter 5 analyses some of the differences and similarities between the systems, and points to some of the implications of these differences.

The four chapters of Section Three look in detail at some of the most important themes that arose from our research. Chapter 6 considers the inter-relationship of structure, culture, ideology and the functioning of different systems giving examples from the discussions with social workers in the countries that we studied. Chapter 7 develops the idea that different perspectives give us a different understanding by looking at a specific example, that of child centred practice as understood in different countries.

Chapter 8 looks at differences and similarities in social work ideology and practice, and relates this to the cultures and structures within which practice takes place. Chapter 9 analyses the way in which our research participants' view of a particular (hypothetical) case expressed a relationship betweeen the state and the family. This was significantly different in each country and very influential in determining the functioning of the child protection system.

Section Four consists of a single chapter, Chapter 10, in which we summarise the messages that we have drawn from this research and look for ways in which the perspectives from other countries can help us in redrawing the patterns of the English system.

The Glossary covers all foreign terms and their translations, and gives brief definitions of the most important English organisations and institutions to which we have made reference.

We have consciously referred throughout to England, not England and Wales because all our research took place in England and we would not assume that there are no differences between England and Wales even though they share the same legislation. We have rarely used 'Britain', or 'the UK', and when we have, it has been with reference to England and Scotland together (usually in comparison with continental Europe).

# Section One:
# The Context of
# Research

In this part we look at the context of the research from which this book originated. Chapter 1 articulates a vision of the relationship between cross-national research, policy change and practice endeavour. Chapter 2 examines the relationship between child protection and the way that society conceives itself. By way of illustration, the functioning of one particular continental system is explored and compared with that of the English system.

# Chapter 1:
# Alternative visions

"What we make of other people, and what we see in the mirror when we look at ourselves, depends on what we know of the world, what we believe to be possible, what memories we have, and whether our loyalties are to the past, the present or the future. Nothing influences our ability to cope with the difficulties of existence so much as the context in which we view them; the more contexts we can choose between, the less do the difficulties appear to be inevitable and insurmountable. The fact that the world has become fuller than ever of complexity of every kind may suggest at first that it is harder to find our way out of our dilemmas, but in reality the more complexities, the more crevices there are through which we can crawl. I am searching for the gaps people have not spotted, for the clues they have missed."

Theodore Zeldin, *An Intimate History of Humanity* (1995).

This book is published at a particular and important moment in the history of child care and protection work in England and Wales. We cannot know how radical the refashioning of systems and practices now in train will turn out to be, but if one thing is certain it is that change is occurring. The book is written first and foremost as a contribution to the process of change, and this introduction attempts to articulate a view about the nature of change in social life and social policy and its links to research, practice and politics. In a rather loose weave, several key themes inform this introduction, and the spirit in which the authors would like the whole book to be received. They are:

- the continuing struggle to implement the radical vision of the Children Act 1989;
- the importance of recovering an ability to think new, creative

4

and even dangerous thoughts in pursuit of change and re-invigoration in child protection work;

- as a stimulus to fresh thinking, a belief in the value of an open-minded response to 'difference' in the experience of how other countries' child welfare institutions work and how their practitioners think and act;
- the opportunity to re-examine and reconstruct the philosophy and character of the central institutions of English social work with children and families;
- the importance of finding strategies which aid the recovery of professional confidence among social workers working with children and families, and in the conception of the total task involved;
- in a general climate of renewed theorisation of what it means to be 'political', to reclaim an understanding of child protection work as a political activity which unites concern for individuals and families with the project of generating social cohesion;
- a view of research as participatory, reflexive, and a medium for rather than a precondition of change.

'Child protection' has no single or fixed meaning in Britain or England, and in the continental countries we studied the concept does not enjoy the same centrality within the overall discourse of social work or child welfare as it does in the UK. Increasing focus on international dimensions of child abuse, particularly organised paedophilia and 'sex tourism' may be creating the beginnings of a common language between anglophone countries and the continent. As this book was being written, details of the abductions and child deaths in a house in southern Belgium were unfolding in the world's media. The present book does not address this or other aspects of child abuse which have impressed themselves on professional and public attention recently, such as institutional regimes of abuse in English and Welsh children's homes. Our focus is more on the everyday task of child protection as it is carried out by social workers and others in community settings. Although we take account of the multi-disciplinarity of child protection systems in all the countries studied, the research and analysis presented here is primarily from a social work perspective.

However, the Belgian crisis of 1996 may be hugely significant. We are often asked 'What is the media attitude to social work and child protection in other European countries?'; 'Do they have public enquiries into child deaths?'; 'Has there been anything comparable to Cleveland?' The very short answers to these questions are respectively, 'On the whole friendly', 'No' and 'No'.

Although there have been some public enquiries in Scandinavia, to our knowledge, no event on the continent has so far led to the politicisation of child abuse and protection issues and installed them in the public domain in the way we have come to take for granted in Britain. One chapter of an earlier book, *Positive Child Protection: A View from Abroad* (Cooper *et al.*, 1995) was devoted to trying to explain this difference. But it is clear that this may all be about to change in Belgium, and there is widespread professional anxiety about the consequences of the 'Dutroux affair' for the child welfare system, parts of which we examine in considerable detail in Chapter 2. If Cleveland installed in the British public mind an unwelcome awareness of the general prevalence of child sexual abuse, the fracturing of public confidence in Belgium is along slightly different lines. The story unfolded rapidly to embrace a murdered former deputy prime minister, organised crime and Mafia involvement, and the arrest of large numbers of police officers and some elected officials. One writer observed that, "...in Belgium today every suspicion appears to be part of the mass trauma: such is the atmosphere that commentators appear to believe it portends some fatal rupture in the state itself." (Helm, 1996, p.2). One main theme of the present book is the need for a more secure political and administrative environment offering a space in which the complex relationship between citizens, professionals, and legal authority in family welfare can be negotiated. This is what appeared to have been achieved in Flanders, and which is now threatened.

## Social spaces

Recent developments in English policy imply a fundamental rethink about the relationship between the concepts of 'children in need', 'child protection', 'family support' and 'child care'. A central thesis of the book is that this reconceptualisation also implies a reconstruction of thinking in terms of the 'social space' occupied by different kinds of interventions in family life. In essence we believe that over the last fifteen years in Britain and especially England, the evolution of political and social life including child protection practice, has resulted in a severe constriction of social space. In the other countries we have studied the preservation of an *intermediate space* between the administrative and judicial spheres, the state and civil society, is reflected and preserved by the structured presence of *intermediate institutions* or *roles* which alleviate many of the acute dilemmas and contradictions of everyday practice experienced by English workers and families. In turn the presence of this 'space' alters the assumptions underpinning voluntary intervention and is capable of strengthening the authority of professionals working in partnership with families in a voluntary capacity. This is about a different meaning of 'space' – one in which the assumptions underpinning practice allow *time* for full assessments on the basis of a proper engagement with families in inherently conflictual and risk-laden situations. The working out of a new and meaningful relationship between children in need, family support and protection implies the reclamation and reconceptualisation of such spaces. As we show in Chapter 2, robust and purposeful child protection work undertaken on the basis of confidentiality and voluntary engagement may be dependent on the nature of what happens when the *limits* of voluntary intervention are reached. Efforts in this direction are represented by the growth of interest in family group conferences and mediation services, but the crucial question is whether and how the structuring of such a space can be guaranteed. The recovery of professional confidence in the child protection field depends not just on whether the media decide to adopt a less accusatory or more considered stance towards child abuse tragedies, but on our capacity to create a socially *protected* (but still accountable) domain in which everyone – children, parents, professionals – find room to breathe, think, negotiate, plan, in the middle of the intensely complex and often long-term process of working out optimum solutions in cases of child abuse.

Marsh and Fisher (1992) describe the growth of a 'third mandate' in child protection work between voluntary agreement and legal compulsion, deriving its authority from regulation and procedure and implemented largely through the agency of the child protection conference. This is a helpful analysis, but we part company with them at the point they introduce principles for working in partnership within areas of this mandate. In our view child protection work must frequently entail the use of authority short of legal compulsion, but we see no reason why such authority has to be derived only from regulatory or administrative sources. As many of the practices in other European countries we describe show, this authority may derive from a *social* mandate, and be reflected in forms of social representation and connectedness embodied by the institutions put in place to manage child welfare cases. These seem to function in turn to support the social mandate with which practitioners carry with them into voluntary partnership with families.

The discovery that relatively protected and socially mandated spaces exist in other European countries' systems, provides a starting point for thinking about the task of change and recovery in our own country. The point is well summed up by one English practitioner who said, "I don't know whether children are better or worse protected in these other countries, but I do think the job of being a child protection worker would be easier than here."

## The tide of change

This book is the product of a process of team research and intellectual enquiry into the character of eight European child protection systems in Belgium (the Flemish and Francophone communities), England, France, Germany, Italy, the Netherlands, and Scotland. This process unfolded over a period of four years, but the outcome cannot be understood in abstraction from a number of contextual factors which inform its perspectives and arguments. One is an earlier book, *Positive Child Protection: A View from Abroad* (Cooper *et al.*, 1995), to which two of the present authors contributed. In that book we used detailed comparison of the French and English child protection systems with the main aim of illuminating the character of the latter, including what seemed to us to be some of its chronic difficulties. The research for that book was undertaken just as the Children Act 1989 came into force in 1991.

By the time the book was published there was a strong feeling in the profession that much of the spirit of the Act was still struggling to find expression. In particular the possibility of truly investing the concept of 'partnership' with substantial meaning seemed to be constricted by a number of structural and cultural obstacles to change. Deep professional and public anxiety surrounding child protection work; the failure to properly reform the family courts system; continued adherence to a highly regulated, centralised, proceduralised and corporatist conception of how to implement a new piece of social legislation; the demoralisation of the social work profession and above all the underfunding of services — all conspired to create a situation in which professionals were in receipt of confused signals, not from the Children Act 1989 itself, but from the continuing influence of the climate of public and professional anxiety which partly occasioned it. "Work in partnership but don't take risks, investigate where there is suspicion but optimise the strengths in families to avoid controlling interventions", and so on. Professional and local political instincts remained understandably conservative, and defensive practices continued despite the legitimation for change provided by the new legislation. The surviving radical vision of the Act was being throttled by 'cultural drag' and an opportunity was becoming transformed into a problem.

The sudden and marked shift in the professional and political climate of English child protection work which began in 1994 more or less coincided with the publication of *Positive Child Protection*. Ideas from abroad seemed to take on a new resonance for professionals, no longer as objects of detached curiosity but as a potential source of meaningful possibilities to inform change at home. Whether we liked it or not (although we did) *Positive Child Protection* became a small current in a changing tide. As a result we found ourselves energetically engaged in contemporary debates about change to the English and Welsh system, even as we continued with the methodical business of researching the character of another six European countries' approaches to child protection. This encouraged us to go on researching and thinking, but also consolidated the meaning and purpose of what we thought we were doing. As a research team we had become aware that the process of research changed us, and changed the practitioners who generated much of the data. For both, the encounter with 'difference' led to systematic reflection on our own thinking and practice and revealed their hidden assumptions, contradictions, confusions and value commitments with a new clarity. This altered state of mind, openness to self-examination and doubt about the grounds of professional belief and practice, suddenly appeared to be the condition which had been lacking in order for the spirit of the Children Act 1989 to come alive.

The live debate in England thus informed the thinking presented in this book, and along the way altered our view not just of English practice and policy, but also of the other systems. From the standpoint of a hypothetical 'pure' research programme, this might sound problematic, for how can you properly compare mutating objects of investigation? Of course, the question only makes sense if child protection systems and practices are conceived as static, rather than as processes which exemplify more or less stable recurrent patterns (structure). Change is always occurring inside a social system, however stable, and whether one researches from the perspective of stability or change is a theoretical choice of some significance.

It is part of the assumption of the book that child protection work in any country at any time is the expression of a system of meanings which are produced, reproduced and modified through time as much by those who undertake the day to day slog, as by the managers, mandarins and ministers who may set policy. Thus an essential source of data for all the countries we studied, including England, were a set of semi-structured conversations among ordinary practitioners in response to a fixed stimulus — a four part case study. We also studied documents, observed and talked informally to practitioners and other researchers, read learned articles and consulted the statute books. But as we brought groups of English practitioners into contact with their continental counterparts, and vice versa (the methodology is described in detail in Chapter 3), we were in fact as interested in the process of change which this occasioned as in the fixed character of the 'meanings' they produced in response to the case study. This change was produced by reflection on the 'difference' between participants' own responses and those of their foreign counterparts. Perhaps this process resulted in nothing more than an interesting day out for these practitioners, giving rise to some interesting thoughts. But nevertheless, what was revealed in each group was the connection between meaning, reflection, understanding, and practice behaviour, in the context of a set of explicit or implicit assumptions about what constitutes 'child protection'.

Each set of conversations originating within the different countries, allied to an understanding of the social institutions through which child welfare is managed and the cultural assumptions informing their character, represents an alternative vision of how the project of child protection might be conceived, understood, implemented and negotiated. Our working assumption is that in any country, a particular instance of practice behaviour only makes sense when understood in the total context of the welfare system in which it is embedded.

In one sense then the material in this book is the product of the reflections of these groups of practitioners, synthesised with the equivalent reflections of the research team, and organised into coherent themes and categories. The descriptive accounts of aspects of systems are important, but we would not want the reader to fasten onto these as in some way representing fact or truth or hard as opposed to soft data. We believe the pictures we present are plausible, free from gross inaccuracy, and would gain the assent of practitioners in the various countries. But our principal hope is that they are themselves a stimulus to new thinking, fresh conceptualisation, creative transposition, imaginative planning in the space which has now opened up, and which we hope remains open, within the English context.

## Resources for change

The impetus towards change signalled by the Audit Commission report *Seen But Not Heard* (1994), and the DOH research findings summarised in *Messages from Research* (Dartington Social Research Unit, 1995) continues as we write now. The nature of the research and thinking presented in this book is in some important respects fundamentally different from any of the studies included in the DOH programme. It is worthwhile to comment on this, because it may help the reader to use the rest of the book to best advantage. We have not set out to prove a thesis, confirm or disconfirm a hypothesis, measure any outcomes, evaluate interventions, classify behaviours or do any of the other things which researchers are usually supposed to do. While we do describe and report data of various kinds, in the end we are concerned to provide raw material for, and provisional interpretations of, ways of seeing the social world in terms of the project of child protection. The central preoccupation is to encourage professional vigour in pursuit of change and betterment of the English system, through the use of creative thought. In examining seven other European child protection systems, we have held up seven mirrors to the English system, and each time seen new things reflected back. These may be ways of thinking, doing, organising, conceptualising, valorising, or processing. The space which has now opened up to think about change in England is both bounded and free. How much freedom there proves to be may be largely a function of how much creativity and energy is liberated to think new thoughts. We want the ideas, interpretations, models of practice presented in this book to be above all *resources for change*.

## Openness to difference

Thus, reading this book might be approached in much the same spirit as an exploratory visit to a site of innovative or good practice in England. The hope is to return with some new ideas which can be transposed and adapted to the home situation. The difference with this book concerns the radicalism, from an English point of view, of the assumptions informing many of the institutions and practices it describes. When we have presented case studies from other countries to English practitioners, the response has usually been a mixture of excitement, shock and anxiety. Occasionally the effect has been sufficiently potent to produce quite gross distortions in the perception of the material. The facts as presented have been too difficult to assimilate and some participants have reworked them to fit their familiar categories of understanding. Extreme reactions of this kind would be unexpected while examining new or different practices within England or probably the UK. Despite wide variations in ways of doing things, these fall within a known and predictable range which constitute the shared cultural framework of our practice. By and large, the research studies within the DOH programme do not challenge or question this framework, and ask and answer questions within assumptive limits which are hidden from view, because they are taken for granted. 'Outcomes' is one example of a concept so much a part of the orthodox canon, that to question its value is almost to speak heresy. Yet few if any of the continental practitioners or researchers we encountered worked with any concept of an 'outcome' as it is understood in Britain now. Whether their child protection systems are better or worse for this, we do not necessarily conclude. But certainly they are different, and it is *openness to difference*, a willingness to absorb and digest the shock of the new rather than reject and recategorise it, which may reward the reader.

## Revolutionary science

The distinction just outlined can be compared to that which the late Thomas Kuhn advanced in his path-breaking work *The Structure of Scientific Revolutions* (1970). Kuhn wrote of the difference between 'normal' and 'revolutionary' science. In his view everyday or 'normal' scientific research is concerned with the business of problem-solving within the limits of a set of prevailing theoretical assumptions about the structure of the world, and the kinds of explanations necessary to understand it. Unsolved problems or contradictory findings are seen to derive from insufficient data, incorrect or incomplete research rather than the limitations of the theory. The framework of assumptions or theory within which research and scientific behaviour are conducted, Kuhn called a paradigm. At some point, a new theory or world view is articulated which is capable of explaining everything which the old one explained, and more. In particular, some of the unsolved problems or anomalies within the old paradigm, turn out to be predicted by the new theory, and cease to be 'problems'. The 'paradigm shift' which brings a new, more powerful explanatory model into being, Kuhn calls 'revolutionary science'. Old facts and familiar ideas are now seen in new ways. Fresh avenues of enquiry open up within the new paradigm, and another era of 'normal science' is under way.

Has the world itself changed in this shift or just the way it is seen, according to Kuhn? This question has preoccupied philosophers in a variety of forms since the beginning of recorded thought. Our answer is 'yes' to both questions, because where the social world is concerned, the subject and object of study are too closely linked to be methodologically separated. Research is a social act in which the researched must inevitably be affected. Research in the positivist tradition (and most of the DOH programme must be characterised as such) attempts to control this effect in the interests of scientificity, comparability, and the effort to isolate the variables or causes of social behaviour. The methodologies developed in the course of our research programme take the simple step of accepting the interactive effects of 'researching' and 'being researched' and exploiting the benefits of these effects. The possibility of simultaneously discovering new ideas *and* experiencing a process of change which in turn leads to new ideas in an organic growth, as opposed to a linear model of researching, finding, publishing, policy-making and policy change, is just one of these benefits. To this extent we have no specifiable expectations of the 'outcome' of this research or the reading of this book. *Protecting Children: Messages from Europe* may transpire to be a set of dead letters, or an incitement to revolt, or more probably something in between. But we cannot control its effects. That is up to the readers. Whatever the effects, they are a continuation of the research effort rather than an implementation of it.

If we have a hope as opposed to an expectation, it is that some or all of the ideas in the book will create revolutions in the mind, in the thinking, of some practitioners, managers, policy makers and maybe clients. Part of the sea-change in child protection work involves the transition from a highly centralised and nationally regulated policy framework towards a more devolved, plural, and with luck, locally responsive service that encourages the use of professional judgement by qualified workers. Children's service plans rather than national regulation are the probable new locus of policy direction; how the revision of *Working Together Under the Children Act 1989* (DOH 1991) will be reconciled with 'refocused' services and the new localism remains unclear at the time of writing. How *local* procedures and the professional culture associated with them are modified is a further important, but as yet undecided question. But we believe the key question is whether child protection work continues to be seen as 'just a service'. The conceptions of practice and institutional meaning informing the work of most of the continental systems we studied appeared, by comparison with the idea of 'service delivery', to be deeply political. This sense of the political derived not from explicitly articulated ideology, or sloganising, but from an implicit connectedness between the nature of social life communities and societies, and the role of child protection institutions in sustaining, preserving, repairing and reconstructing what is valued about the wider form of life. This often seemed to be related to a sense of social 'tradition', a stable understanding about the place of family life and children within society, which underlies and survives the sometimes radical disruption and discontinuity of the recent politics of these societies – German reunification being the most marked instance of the latter.

## Reconstructing the political

It is easy to identify and then idealise some feature of an unfamiliar culture, and bemoan the loss of some equivalent in one's own. Nevertheless, the current spate of vigorous retheorising of the political domain by British social theorists — Anthony Giddens (1994), John Gray (1996) and Paul Hirst (1994) to name but a few — is significantly propelled by the recognition that 17 years of Tory government has been devoted to the destruction of tradition. In the view of these writers, this is what marked out Thatcherism and distinguished it from 'old Conservatism'. Traditional social structures and bonds, including many of those which maintained the power of relatively privileged groupings such as the established professions, have been swept aside along with the trade unions and manufacturing industry, to create market freedom. Arguably, these events have bitten far deeper into the fabric of social life in the UK than in most other European countries so far. Although a pale shade of pink when read against the hard left theory of the 1960s or 1970s which informed the 'radical social work' of the time, Will Hutton's *The State We're In* (1996) signals a major reawakening of public interest in the question of social bonds, and their organic relationship to political and economic life. Amongst other themes, Hutton's book is shot through with a fierce critique of compartmentalisation in political and social analysis, which may be transposed to ask awkward but important questions about contemporary social work ideology and practice, and the disjunction between ideals of 'quality', 'user rights', 'empowerment', and the lived experience of children and families who want differentiated, skilful help with deeply damaging life situations.

Child protection work, whether conceptualised in terms of

'family support' or not, always entails a relationship to social, community and political life, and the deployment of socially given authority. Hutton's account of the demolition and constriction of whole layers of intermediate organisation in British life, including local government which is the primary institutional base for organised social work established by Seebohm, alerts us to the impoverished state of the socio-political environment in which child protection work is practised. The child protection conference is the central institution which occupies a middle ground between voluntary and compulsory intervention in family life in England. But how 'social' is it as an institution? By comparison with The Flemish mediation committee, the Scottish children's panel, the French prevention conference, or even the more highly individualised setting of the office of the children's judge in France, Italy, Germany, or Holland, the child protection conference seems poorly integrated with the wider society of the family and the professional.

The project of reconstructing the relationship between professional child protection work, the interests and needs of children, parents and families, and the communities or localities in which problems and their solutions typically arise and are found is timely for several reasons. First, the impetus towards the deregulation of the child protection system and the return to more locally conceived and legitimated services represents an opportunity both for the child protection system and all who have an interest in it, and for wider projects of local political reconstruction to draw strength from and contribute to the complex process of creating conditions of improved social cohesion. Second, the chance is there for social work to secure its endangered position in the range of primary care professions by articulating the political as well as the therapeutic significance of the skills, methods, and models which are its bread and butter. The modes of institutionalised social and political relationship which might inform the 'new politics' of John Gray's *After Social Democracy* (1996), Anthony Giddens' *Beyond Left and Right* (1994) or Paul Hirst's *Associative Democracy* (1994) are actually what every social worker deals in every day of their working life. As Giddens says,

> "Dialogue, between individuals who approach one another as equals, is a transactional quality central to their mutuality. There are remarkable parallels between what a good relationship looks like, as developed in the literature of marital and sexual therapy, and formal mechanisms of political democracy. Both depend on what David Held calls a *principle of autonomy*..." (1994, pp. 118-9).

If social workers began to think of their activities in family centres, day centres, residential homes, and case conferences as a model for micro-political institutions they would discover that their understanding of relationship skills and dynamics already has a strong political dimension. In Europe we have seen a variety of models for how the intermediate 'social space' in which most family support and child protection work occurs might be structured. But quite apart from these, English practitioners have a rich fund of experience and theory on which to draw for the construction of their own.

The programme of study and enquiry on which this book is based began in England, led us (and will take the reader) into other European countries. Our discovery, and we want it to be the reader's also, is that while we set out with the thought of seeing many places through one set of eyes, we finished by seeing one place — England — through the eyes of many.

# Chapter 2:
# Reclaiming social space

In the course of a discussion about child protection procedures, an English social worker in a research group for this study said, "But what do we have to go on in our work, without the procedures?" There are many ways to interpret this comment, and it may represent a view of what professional child protection work is about which would be rejected by most practitioners. Yet, to the extent that all English practitioners are enslaved by the volumes of procedure and regulation which accompany the Children Act 1989 and the everyday child protection task, the remark captures a vital truth. English child protection work has become an administrative routine. It is not a routine which can be performed without skill, judgement, training, knowledge, sensitivity to feelings, as well as all the other elements of what we might call traditional professionalism. An examination of contemporary case files, which are the administrative 'memory' of the system, reveals that these 'old' values and underpinnings survive as part of practice, but clearly *in the service* of the administrative goals of the system. The individual practitioner may still seek and find job satisfaction from other dimensions of the task, and feel that her vocational longings (another 'old' value) can be answered. But vocation, professionalism, reparative drive, commitment to social justice are no longer the sufficient conditions to perform the task. What the social worker's remark captures is that the procedures *legitimate* what he does. One could ask, what about his own capacity to make assessments, his own professional authority, his use of relationships with families and children to guide decision-making, or a host of other possible sources of legitimation for his day to day practice?

The thesis for which we argue in this chapter is that the legitimating context of English child protection work was severely eroded in the decade leading up to 1996, and that this is understandable as an instance of much broader changes in the structure of British society which have laid waste to intermediate social spaces and the institutions which sustained them. Administration, regulation and procedure in the child protection system are what have filled the social vacuum created by this restructuring. We will argue for the need to reconstruct a socially 'protected space' in child welfare if the project of 'rebalancing' or refocusing the child protection system is to have any chance of succeeding in meaningful terms. This project cannot be a simple recovery of 'old' values, methods and structures — one of the most frequently voiced anxieties of the present time is that a return to 'family support' will mean regression to forms of practice which are widely felt to have contributed to the child protection crisis of the 1980s. Rather, the project is to *rethink* in very concrete terms what principles a more fully socialised child protection system would be built upon. The child protection conference is the central social institution in the management of child protection work, and we want to examine its structure and potential as a social institution, through comparison with similar bodies in other European countries. The chapter pays particular attention to the practice and institutions of the Flemish community of Belgium, partly as an entry point to the comparative themes of the book, and partly because the recent history of their system shows the feasibility of the project of 'reclaiming social space'.

## A Flemish child protection case

The referral came to a social worker at *Kind in Nood*, a confidential doctor centre in Leuven, from a social worker in the public health service. She had with her a young woman of 19 called Olivia, living alone, anxious about her younger sister aged 13, who she thought was being sexually abused. Olivia agreed to come and talk to the *Kind in Nood* social worker if she could give a false name.

Olivia said that she was the third child in a family of seven, four girls and three boys. The two youngest were Mark and Theresa, twins of 13. Mark had told her that something wrong was going on between Theresa and their father. Olivia said that she had been sexually abused by their father and that she thought that her two elder sisters had been as well. All three of them had been sexually abused by their paternal grandfather, who had been convicted of abusing his own children. Olivia had told her mother, who said, "never be alone with grandfather", and "perhaps it is true, but I never saw it."

At this point the social worker asked if Olivia could arrange for her to meet with Theresa secretly either at school or at the centre. Theresa came to see her with Mark, who she said tried to protect her. The children did not want the father out of the family, and they did not want to leave themselves. The social worker got the permission of the children to contact the parents in order to try to see them. She arranged with the children that she would contact their parents on the Monday, to give herself room for manoeuvre, and arranged for Theresa to spend that night with Olivia, going straight to her lodgings from school.

On Monday she phoned the mother and asked her to come to the centre, bringing the father with her. She confronted them with her knowledge of the abuse. The mother talked a great deal, evasively, and the father denied the abuse and kept very quiet. After a while, the social worker made the mother leave so that she could talk to the father without the mother intervening. The father denied having abused the children, saying that he had only been tickling them. The social worker responded that she would not be wasting her time on something like that, this was much more serious. She did not accept his description. She arranged for him to come back to see her the next day, told him that Theresa was staying with her elder sister and that he was not to see her or telephone her. She then rang the mother to make a further appointment and apologise for having sent her out of the initial interview.

All the children started to telephone the social worker asking for appointments. None of them wanted the father sent away, and initially they denied having been abused, but when the social worker disagreed, they began to tell her about both physical and sexual abuse.

The parents attended further interviews. They did not get angry, but they could not hear the social worker when she talked about sexual abuse, and could not talk about it or use the words. The father said, "you are strong when you can forget the past." He had been severely abused by his own father as a child; when he was 12 he had told a teacher who said that he could not help. The social worker tried to draw parallels and make connections, but the father could not accept the connections and continued to insist that the abuse was 'just tickling'.

The social worker consulted her multi-disciplinary team in the centre, which included social workers, psychologists, child psychiatrists and family therapists. The team supported her feeling that it was important to get the father to recognise the words 'sexual abuse', and supported her in setting up a family meeting which would be videoed and watched by the team.

The mother said that her father had died when she was 13. She had not had a good relationship with her mother, who blamed her for her father's death. She was put into foster care, where she was abused by the nephew of her carers, and raped. She equated sexual abuse with rape. She felt that if her husband left, it would be like her father dying all over again. "You can't be a good mother without a father there." During the session the mother laughed and joked with her daughters. At one point, the father said "I shouldn't have done those things." The social worker had to ask the mother several times whether she had heard what the father had said.

There were many points at which the social worker considered taking Theresa out of the household, but she decided against this, helped in reaching her decision by the reflections of the centre team. Work continued with the whole family with the younger children and both parents still at home. She did not have to involve any other agency in her work, though if she had decided on a different approach, she might have needed to go to the mediation committee which we describe below, or, if she had thought the situation sufficiently dangerous, made an emergency referral to the public prosecutor.

## Working in space

A short case illustration always asks more questions than it answers. Even on the basis of the limited information presented above, many English practitioners will react with surprise, concern or shock at the handling of the disclosures. When the case was presented in this form to a large group of English workers, the material also seemed to generate anxiety and hostility from some, and distortions of the content. This is an understandable response, since the narrative is being received and processed as though it was an *English* case, for which the worker is responsible. For the moment we want to concentrate less on the details of the practice, more on a dispassionate consideration of what kind of approach is illustrated here, and what makes it possible.

The worker in this case is a highly trained family therapist, and it is evident that her response is primarily a 'whole family' one. In discussion of her work she says, "You must give time to time", which is to say, the process of working towards particular objectives such as protecting the children from further abuse while taking account of the complex family dynamics, takes time. *Process is balanced with, but possibly also in tension with, the outcome.*

She also says, "I need my anxiety to work", which is to say the children's predicament makes her anxious and is a stimulus to intervention, but also a recognition that it is tempting to alleviate anxiety rather than let it work in the service of a process of work with the family. She has no procedures to reassure her that she is 'doing the right thing', but she does have a team who she turns to for consultation and support. Presumably she would listen to them if they disagreed strongly with her approach. *Professional trust rather than managerial direction is a key source of legitimation and accountability in her day to day decisions.*

She intervenes using authority, confidence, and an appreciation of the dynamic consequences of her 'directiveness'. She over-rides 'parental responsibility' in order to offer immediate 'protection' to Theresa, but on the understanding both that the child needs her help to confront the parents, and that as soon as possible Theresa will be 're-connected' to the family in the way that she wishes. The various potential conflicts of rights and responsibilities in this situation cannot be handled unless the worker is confident she can 'give time to time' and knows that she is authorised to hold these tensions in balance through the course of time. *Professional confidence and authority are linked by their relationship to a legitimated 'space' in which they are allowed to function.*

Intervention is not just as an example of family therapy or a case of sexual abuse, but a conflictual and contested social situation involving many dimensions. Parents, adult children living away from home, minors still living at home, an involved social welfare agency, the mediation committee and the courts in the background, personal and social history (the parents' own experience of abuse) can all be playing a continuing active role. In this context, the social worker's intervention can be seen as a complex effort to provoke conflict by confronting the parents, in the attempt to restructure power relations in the family in favour of the children, while keeping all parties actively engaged with and connected to one another. She demonstrates her own involvement in this, by first removing the mother from an interview, but later apologising and repairing the connection. *Working in partnership with children and parents means working with, and possibly exacerbating conflict, while sustaining rather than sundering their continued relationships.*

The social worker saw this case as an illustration of how she was able to work in a way which allowed the children to retain control. Clearly this entailed her 'taking charge' of the relationship with the parents. But the children do not want to leave home, or the 'perpetrator' to leave either, and so she works on this basis. In

England the 'duty to protect the individual child' might frequently lead to their wishes being overridden in such circumstances. As we show in Chapter 7 'child-centredness' is not a straightforward concept. But in this context child-centredness, the duty to protect the rights and responsibilities of parents, the rights and responsibilities of children, and the ambiguities of children's attachments to abusing parents, are able to be seen as a complex configuration which is amenable to change over time through skilled intervention, rather than the object of an administrative calculus. *Child-centredness is a principle with multiple meanings depending on context, and will have differential applications according to context.*

The 'space' in which this case is worked has limits, alluded to in the mention of the mediation committee and the public prosecutor. It is easy to confuse the idea of space, and its limits, which we are advancing here, with that of 'thresholds'. If the Flemish social worker reached the point where she believed that the interests or protection of the children could no longer be preserved or secured through her work, or conflicts within the family or between herself and family members proved intractable, then she would take the decision to refer the situation to the mediation committee. But this would not be simply on the grounds of an assessment of the 'severity of the abuse'; rather it would be a function of the state of play in the total configuration of the family *and* her own involvement. The degree of parental and child co-operation, her own and her team's skills and resources, new information, the degree of therapeutic leverage, and many other factors might contribute to a decision to approach the committee. But most importantly, she and her colleagues are judged to be competent to work with the situation, and competent to decide when the limits of their competence (and that of the family's) to resolve the situation have been reached. This is the principle of subsidiarity in operation. The work described above does not occur 'beneath a threshold' but within a domain of socially legitimated competence, within which professionals are given a comparatively free hand. Their sense of professional identity clearly extends beyond abiding by a professional code, to include active understanding of their position within a wider system of social responsibility, meaning and accountability.

One could ask of the above case, what if the children had been younger? How then does the system enable children to stay in control? In our experience no system suggests easy or automatic answers to questions like this, but the following short case study illustrates how the matter was addressed in one case drawn from a service in Luxembourg, which has adopted the same system as the French-speaking Belgian community.

## A child protection case from Luxembourg

A Francophone Belgian social worker and family therapist who works in a child and family service in Luxembourg described a case in which the revelation of sexual abuse by a father of his six year old twin daughters, resulted in an arrangement whereby the father's new partner who had experienced child sexual abuse herself, acted as 'protector' in subsequent meetings between father and children. The service trusted this solution which was found by the family group, partly because of the woman's personal experience. The twins were worked with in an intensive programme by a team psychologist, and amongst other things enabled them to speak directly to the father about how they had experienced his abuse, and what they would wish by way of 'reparation'. This transpired to be that should either of them experience any future educational or emotional difficulty, he would pay for remedial or therapeutic services. The mother decided that she would press charges against the father, but in the end the gendarmerie recommended that he should not be prosecuted since he was no longer an active danger to his children, and had admitted his guilt. The children's judge concurred with this decision.

Listening to this social worker describing her work with the case, there is a strong impression of formal and informal authority (the police, the judge, the social worker) operating in harness with an effort to keep authority and control in the family, supported by the professionals. The family group elects its own 'protector', and past events, present crisis, and future implications are brought into relationship through the reparative agreement — the message is that the family unit cannot escape the consequences and future impact of what has happened, and that punishment by itself will not amount to justice. The compensatory agreement attempts to link elements of adult responsibility and reparation, wrong deeds and their consequences, and bring children's 'rights' into a meaningful connection with their powerlessness and potential for empowerment. The father is not prosecuted, but he may have to endure longer term public reminders of his past deeds than if he had served a prison sentence. The *meaning* of his actions for his children and family are addressed as much as the wrongfulness of what he did. All of this could have been different, had the father not acknowledged his guilt, or the mother insisted harder on a prosecution, or the abuse been more serious than it actually was, or any one of a number of other factors. The handling of the case represents a form of 'negotiated justice', and has something in common with the culture of French child protection work in which children's judges, social workers, children and parents will attempt to work out solutions in the space offered by the *audience* in the judge's office (Cooper *et al.*, 1995).

This view of the child protection task as configurative, systemic, contextual and processional leads to one inevitable objection — arbitrariness. Surely different families and children in comparable circumstances will be subjected to different interventions, including the use of more or less coercion, unless there is some agreed standard or common measure of when to move across 'thresholds'. The problem of finding a bridge between conceptualisations of the child protection task which start from an aggregated appreciation of the multi-variate, context and process dependent nature of a case, and those which begin by disaggregating the variables in a range of cases in search of common trends, are considerable and by no means confined to child protection. In Britain there has perhaps been a particular problem in holding both methodologies equally in mind, allowing the quite different intellectual 'paradigms' and value systems they represent to interact in a fruitful way. Thus for example, the concept of 'a threshold' can easily be mistaken as a guide to future intervention in individual cases, when it is only capable of functioning as a tool for retrospective analysis of patterns of behaviour within a system. Whether apocryphal or true, stories of local authority social service departments achieving rapid and drastic reductions in the numbers of children on their child protection registers illustrate the dangers of misapplying survey analysis to the project of system change. Equally, a narrow and unchecked reliance on 'good practice' principles to achieve system objectives might realise the anxieties of those who fear a 'return to the 1950s'. In our study, English practitioners were consistently impressed by the freedom and confidence in autonomous professional judgement manifested by practitioners from many of the continental countries, but equally concerned to know how 'bad practice' or practice standards in general were monitored and regulated.

This response by English practitioners must, of course, be seen against the familiar background of recent history in which some instances of 'bad practice' have been blamed for child death, and led to vehement ensuing social disapprobation. If poor practice has catastrophic consequences, then the incentive to monitor and eliminate it becomes of paramount importance. This as much as anything explains English social workers' love-hate relationship with child protection procedures. While in place, they are frequently an object of frustration, derision, and attack. But contemplate their removal, and what is revealed is the image of a dead child. Thus, the question of how 'failure' in child protection work, including child death, is viewed becomes of central importance. During a seminar (Cooper *et al.*, 1996) in which French, Flemish and German practitioners presented examples of their practice to small groups of English child protection workers, the continental workers were struck by the fact that the same question had arisen in all three groups — how many children die as a result of abuse each year in your country? Not only did they not know the answer, the question did not resonate with any of them in the way it does in England, because measures of serious incidents do not function as primary indicators of professional, public or political evaluations of the efficacy of their child protection systems. However, child death in the context of the delivery of public child welfare services is by no means unknown or unrecognised in these countries. As we shall see, child death and 'failures' in the system occupied a place in the thinking which lead to the construction and consolidation of a socially legitimated 'intermediate sphere' in the Flemish system, but in the context of a very different system of meanings which attached to them.

## Constructing social space — the sphere of voluntary intervention in Flanders

In the late 1980s, following the reformation of Belgium as a federal state, the Flemish community of Belgium began to develop its own services and legislation in relation to child welfare and child protection. This had to build on and accommodate the existing legislative and court structure which was determined by the Belgian Federal Government. In 1985 and 1990 the Flemish community passed new legislation that made major changes in the structures and the approach to services for children and families. In many respects their aims were similar to those of the Children Act 1989, but the product was considerably different. They were unable to change the court structure or the powers of the courts in relation to children and families (which are federal powers), but the changes they made at the stage preceding court referral were extensive and significant.

The provision of Belgian social services is based on the

subsidiary principle. The effect of this is that there are many small voluntary organisations offering a range of help, and a rather limited generic local social services system. This is the starting point for most families, although some will go directly to the second stage of specialist help. The specialist service is called the Committee for Special Youth Assistance and was set up by the law of 1985. It is responsible for providing a service for individual work with children and young people where there is a 'problematic educational situation'. (Ministry of the Flemish Community, 1995) An alternative translation of this phrase is 'problematic up-bringing situation', which may give a more accurate impression. The concern is not about education as we use the word in Britain, but about the general health, welfare and development of the child or young person. The Social Services for Special Youth Assistance work on a voluntary basis. It offers support, counselling, and other services either through its own social workers or through other agencies. They have a duty to see that suitable services are available.

The voluntary nature of this is important, and there is an emphasis on the fact that this service is not a service for the courts. As we have indicated, one of the changes made in the new legislation was to separate voluntary intervention with families from statutory intervention. The general importance for the Flemish community of working on a voluntary basis is also illustrated by the strength of the development of the confidential doctor centres, described by one social worker in the service as neither medical nor confidential. This service offers to work with families suffering abuse on a basis of confidentiality; they do not guarantee that they will *never* invoke the law, but they will go further than other organisations in trying to work without doing so, and consider that they are nearly always able to do this. They also offer confidentiality to anyone telling them about abuse to a child.

Writing about the recent evolution of the voluntary sphere of the Flemish system and the problem of balancing 'help and control' in the context of Flanders' old child abuse centres, Catherine Marneffe says:

> "The therapeutic model of the confidential doctor centre was developed in 1986 in response to some difficulties within the system. Although child abuse centres received most families in a therapeutic environment, without cases having to be reported by law, it was also a context where help and control were delicately balanced, provoking tremendous tensions between

families and professionals. In fact the centres used to call upon the courts whenever therapy was not working, which was very often (30% of the cases). Parents were aggressive, they refused to come to the out-patient department, workers were depressed and tired, and children were often kept at home against medical advice."

"These tensions were such that they resulted in failures, with dramatic consequences for the children including re-injuries and even death. A pre-natal follow-up survey conducted in 1985 of 374 children, considered at risk before their birth, showed that four children died within a therapeutic programme. Analysis of these failures and the 'burn-out' syndrome among workers highlighted the duality of what is expected of professionals — balancing a role as therapist helping the family, and a role as social controllers of acceptable behaviours. This dual role put both professionals and families in a 'no win' situation for several reasons." (1992, p.23).

The date mentioned by Marneffe, 1986, is significant if we want to compare the parallel developments of the Flemish and English system, read off against the common background of a recognition of 'failures' and child death. In England the response to the series of public enquiries of the mid-1980s led in one direction, while the project of reconstruction in Flanders went in quite another. As we argue below, this must be explained partly in terms of divergences in the broader political and social evolution of the two countries, but ten years on in the climate of re-evaluation in England there may be significant lessons for this country as we turn our attention to the coming decade. Arguably, the same difficulty in balancing the 'care and control' dimensions of the child protection task were a root cause of the crisis which swept over the English system. In Flanders the response to this structural difficulty in the system was two fold:

*To effect a clearer separation of the two domains, and create an intermediate zone in which difficult cases could be assessed and managed.*

In England the response, though largely unplanned, was:

*To extend control to more and more families, via a framework of investigation regulation, procedure and through the child protection conference system, which moved 'therapeutic' intervention to one side.*

In crude terms, the outcome of this in England is accurately portrayed by the findings of the Audit Commission (1994) and Gibbons et al., (1995) that large numbers of children were being

drawn into the system who did not need formal protection, and
that a high proportion of these were receiving no follow-up. This is
the concrete manifestation of the evolution of Marsh and Fisher's
(1992) 'third mandate'. King and Piper (1990) and King and
Trowell (1992) have analysed respectively the 'colonisation' of
welfare discourse by legal discourse, and the incompatibility of the
legal and welfare paradigms which were revealed as the 'space' in
which these tensions were once negotiated dissolved and was
reconstructed in terms of administrative and procedural imperative.

Marneffe (1992) is eloquent and passionate in her support for
the full legitimation of a 'medico-social model' of child abuse
understood as a result of family dysfunction, contrasted with a
'judicial model' in which "abuse and neglect of the child by his or
her parents are considered a criminal offence and the first solution
is to punish and penalise the perpetrators". She produces figures
to show that following the establishment of the service: self-
referrals by abusing families increased; that a very high proportion
of perpetrators recognised the abuse without threat from the
courts; a high proportion of children and families stay in treatment
and so on. The passion which informs her analysis is the same as
that which motivates the Flemish worker involved in the case
described earlier in this chapter. It is a belief in the potency of a
well-trained professional sure of her values with respect to abuse
and abusers, capable of holding acute conflicts in a constructive
tension, to confront abuse, protect children, and work through the
family dynamics to an optimum resolution. Marneffe mentions,
almost as an aside, that in an analysis of 110 cases, judicial
authorities were needed in only six per cent and that these were
referred to the juvenile court (1992). More families and more
perpetrators come forward for help, and more children are better
protected if confidentiality is assured — that is the basis of her
position.

The downplaying of the significance of the role of law and other
forms of socially legitimated authority in the Flemish system as a
whole is rather characteristic of the Flemish practitioners who
work in the voluntary sphere. It derives from a perception which
sees judicial intervention as having actually contributed to abuse in
the past. As one writer observes, there is "a mistrust, bordering on
abhorrence, for the judicial system's handling of child sexual
abuse". One doctor, a team co-ordinator in the confidential doctor
centre, is cited as follows: "I have known many court cases which
have been tragic for the children — where they have been under
such pressure their stories have changed repeatedly and the whole

thing has gone on for months with so much animosity that it is an abuse in itself". (Neate, 1991) Another child psychiatrist has spoken thus:

> "...it's so hard to prove sexual abuse that it's less painful not to bother. Verdicts are so capricious as to depend on who is the judge that day."
>
> "Last year we had a child who had been raped by her father. She was so badly injured she had to have two blood transfusions. We had to bring the case to court because the mother didn't believe her child so we wouldn't work with the family. This girl was five years old. She was interviewed in court from 10am until 4pm. At 3.30pm they brought in her father and she said: 'Oh no.' The police said: 'Why do you say that? It's not true, what you said is it?' She said: 'It's true but I love my daddy.' So they said: 'He may go to prison you know. Do you really want to do this?'
>
> "A while ago when we took a child into hospital and the father objected I used to tell him if he didn't let the chil stay, I would involve the police. Now I say, 'If you want to get your child, you go and get the police.' I'm showing them, if they want repression they can have it, but we want to work with them." (Neate, 1991).

However, as we have seen, this perspective is not part of an inherently 'anti-authority' stance. These workers use their own authority in alliance with therapeutic skill to confront and work through abuse in families. Some of the events this doctor describes and abhors are familiar in England, and gave rise to the *Memorandum of Good Practice* (1992). But in so far as the *Memorandum* was an important attempt to protect children from the worst experiences of giving evidence in court, it was also an accommodation to the system. The different trajectories of development of the Flemish and English systems, are different answers to the central question of how to manage the tension between 'help and control': piecemeal reform or global restructuring?

Yet it is clear (although Marneffe and others underplay the overall significance of this) that confidentiality is not an absolute guarantee in the system. It is equally clear, as we have tried to indicate, that the 'space' in which these practitioners function is *dependent* upon the availability of other forms of authority which operate *as the boundary of this space*. Some cases cannot be worked with, some conflicts cannot be resolved, in some instances time and skill and passion are not enough. What happens then?

## Constructing social space — the mediation committee and emancipating authority

"The tasks of the commission of mediation can be seen as a tryptich. It has to function as a *buffer* for cases that threaten to flow from assistance to judicial intervention. This flow has to be *filtered:* only in extreme cases can it be appropriate to filter a dossier to the juvenile court. The commission of mediation is also an *alternative* to judicial action: public prosecutors can now call in the commission of mediation instead of the juvenile court."

(de Cauter, 1995)

"First we invite the person who made the referral, because we want to listen very carefully to the reasons why they approached the commission. Then the commission, independently of anyone else, decides which people they want to invite. The commission thinks very carefully about who to communicate with, so if it's the social worker who has approached us, then we see the social worker first, then the young people, the parents, maybe other social workers in the home where the young people are staying; or a doctor, someone in whom they have confidence, a friend...In that conference we try to work out a solution which everybody can agree to."

An Sprangers, mediation committee member (Hetherington and Sprangers, 1994).

The Committee for Special Youth Assistance described earlier in this chapter was a major innovation for the Flemish system, but the mediation committee represented a greater departure, and seems to be something very rare in organisational change, a new invention. There is a mediation committee in each judicial area, consisting of six members who are government appointees. They are people with some specialist knowledge of problematic educational situations. The committee meets twice a month, and can be convened at any time in an emergency. Its function is to mediate between social workers and families (parents and/or children) where the process of social work help has broken down and no progress is being made, but where one side or the other feel that help is still needed. They act as a neutral buffer zone between the failure of work on a voluntary basis and the courts.

The committee can be approached either by the social worker from the special youth assistance service or other recognised services, by the parents, or by the child or young person. Social workers can approach the committee if the help offered is being refused; parents or children can approach the committee if help is refused or if they do not agree with what is provided; and parents can also go to the committee when they have serious problems with their children's behaviour.

The child has the right to be included in discussions with the mediation committee. If a plan is made, any child of 14 or over has to consent to the plan. Children can claim a right to assistance and can refuse it. The plans worked out in discussion with the mediation committee have a specific duration and are only extended if their aims have not been met and there is a further agreement to continue.

The committee aims to find an agreed solution. If they are not able to do so, they can either decide that the matter is not serious enough to warrant compulsory intervention, or they can refer the case to the public prosecutor and thence to court for a judicial decision. If the judge did not find grounds for compulsory action, she would be able to refer the case back to the committee (via the public prosecutor). Except in situations of emergency, only the committee can refer cases to the public prosecutor. It is the gatekeeper of the route to legal intervention.

All the child protection systems we have studied emphasise the importance of prevention and working in partnership, but have different ways of approaching this. The Flemish system seems to have gone furthest in institutionalising prevention and voluntary working so that it is a structural part of their way of working. The dominant concepts informing the work of the mediation committee involve maximising the possibility of working on a voluntary basis and making sure that appropriate help is being offered to children and young people. The fact that parents and children can ask for help from the committee is a very important aspect of its role, and characterises it as neutral and investigative (but not in a judicial sense), and makes a clear statement of the expectation that all parties will be listened to.

In a more dispassionate, but no less principled analysis than that of Marneffe (1992), de Cauter (1995) discusses the fundamental tensions between the role of law and the role of 'assistance' in responding to child welfare problems, tensions which were the motivating force in the decision to construct an intermediate zone between the two. The difficulty which has tended to bedevil British debates of the 'justice and/or welfare', 'care and/or control' type, has been the lack of an *intermediate concept* with which to give meaning and coherence to the formation of a 'buffer zone' between the two. This lack has helped to perpetuate the binary and polarised character of the tensions, and policy debates surrounding them. The 'voluntarism' of voluntary as opposed to statutory intervention thus easily elides with a concept of negative freedom — freedom as freedom from constraint, defined by everything it is not (the control invested in the law), rather than being invested with any positive content. De Cauter introduces the notion of *emancipating authority* and distinguishes this from both judicial power and pure 'voluntarism':

> "The idea of protection (as written in the law of 1965) tends to 'isolate youngsters from social events and deprive them of too much responsibility'. The model of protection is accordingly countered with an emancipatory approach. On the basis of equivalence youngsters should get enough room to develop as well as to realise and enforce their rights. Emancipation is not equal to mere freedom and licentiousness, but rather an awakening to 'one's place and responsibility in society'. As such, emancipation is an essentially interactive event, 'a sense of responsibility in solidarity with others'.
> (de Cauter, 1995 p.7).

The idea of 'solidarity' is important in understanding the socio-political context in which many European child welfare systems are embedded, and is discussed in more detail in Chapter 5. For the moment we need to register that the mediation committee itself embodies, and helps reproduce social 'solidarity' or connectedness, and that the means by which it does this is *dialogue*. The authority for this dialogue to take place derives from the legitimation conferred upon members of the committee themselves through their appointment by government. As 'lay' members of a social institution which is accessible to not just professionals, but also children and parents, and which aims to treat these parties equally, the membbers act to link the proceedings and the authority of the committee to the wider society in which all are citizens. Thus the committee is understood by those involved more as a social organism than an administrative body, and as such its continued evolution, improvement, and integration with the wider social fabric is accepted. Sprangers gives a sense of this:

> "Yes, I believe in the system. There are still some shortcomings that we have to iron out I think, but it's not easy to make changes. Some people feel that mediation should be undertaken by professionals, others prefer it as it is. We are looking at ways to try and improve it, but I believe in the principle of the system."
> "I think the great strength of the commission (is that) they

are not involved. The commission has authority, not judicial or statutory authority, but 'moral' authority, and I hope it has the capacity to unblock some of the difficulties or impasses that can occur in social work."
(Hetherington and Sprangers, 1994).

This brief introduction to the principles informing the mediation committee can serve as a way of reflecting on the potential for the development of such institutions in England. The central ideas, of uniting 'emancipation' with authority and addressing conflicts through the use of dialogue, are by no means unfamiliar to practitioners in this country, and are one way of summarising the main principles of traditional casework. Arguably, the child protection conference was once also conceptualised by some practitioners in a rather similar way — as a demonstration of authority through which 'therapeutic leverage' could be obtained in intractable cases. However, if this is accurate (and it may still represent an aspect of how practitioners think about the role of the conference), it is clear that the two institutions diverge in more respects than they converge, although at first sight the conference appears to occupy a similar 'intermediate zone' in the English system, between 'law' and voluntary intervention. The differences in the two institutions reflect, embody, and reproduce something greater than themselves — the conception and legitimation of the social space they occupy.

- The conference is an *administrative body* rather than a *social institution*, and is defined in order to serve administrative ends rather than social ones. This is reflected in its membership, which does not connect it to wider society.
- Conference membership is *'professional'* rather than *'lay'*.
- Co-ordination, planning, assessment of risk and registration decisions, are the primary responsibilities of the conference. Its role is *decision-making* rather than *mediation or problem-solving*.
- The mode of conduct of relationships in a conference is framed by its *tasks, agenda and orientation to outcome* rather than a focus on communication as a *medium for a process*, which is integral to achieving outcomes.
- The conference is not *accessible* to parents, children, and the wider community in a planned and 'constitutional' manner. It is formed on an ad hoc, case by case basis with a changing membership. This makes 'access' difficult, since there is nothing to gain access to, outside each particular instance of its formation. The conference does not (and cannot) therefore

*receive* referrals from or put itself *at the service of* a population.
- Restricted access is thus a *structural* feature, rather than just one of 'style' or 'culture'. The mediation committee is a *public body*, which is reflected in its membership, and its consequent organic link to the community.
- Although the conference is a multi-disciplinary meeting, in effect it is managed by just one profession, social work, and this further restricts its potential for public, social, and professional *accountability*.

It should be clear then, that the many well-intended, and indeed effective, attempts at reforming the child protection conference in the direction of fuller participation, parental involvement, accountability and so on, have absolute limits set by the roles, tasks and definitions which constitute its *raison d'être*. The mediation committee not only establishes and occupies a particular 'social space', but the kind of things which happen between children, parents, professionals, and committee members on each occasion it meets — literally in the space of the room where the meeting is held — are made possible only because the committee is an institution of a particular kind.

The inherent limitations on reform of the child protection conference are what have given rise to interest in alternatives such as family group conferences and mediation services. But this development is part of a much wider trend towards discovering and experimenting with 'intermediate institutions' in social and political life generally. The mediation committee is a multi-faceted institution, but one face of its being is self-avowedly political, and in so far as it also serves to 'administer' the child welfare system of Flanders, administration is organically tied to political ends. This is an illustration of what differentiates the social context of social work in many continental countries from England. Where services for children are enshrined by the principles of social solidarity, subsidiarity and citizenship, one consequence is that the institutions which organise, deliver and shape local responses to child protection are structured into, and derive their authority from a total conception of society.

The critical question facing the English child protection system as it reviews, re-evaluates and attempts to redefine itself is — 'how can any social consensus, local or national, about the form of new services, be protected and given a chance to develop, flourish and contribute to renewed social cohesion rather than just the narrow project of 'protecting the child' in isolation from its social surroundings?' This is the same question which political theorists of a variety of persuasions are asking about the whole character of British social life. We do not cite the work of Will Hutton and others in order to ally ourselves with any party political position, or with the intention of seducing the reader with a rhetorical strategy, but because there seems to be a deep resonance between the questions which our comparative analysis has made us ask, and the loftier ones which these thinkers pose. Their source is the same, a profound anxiety about the quality of public life, public service, and the meaning of social life for ordinary citizens.

"If the state is careless about its constitution, and thus its relationship with those in whose name it purports to rule, it can hardly be a surprise that such carelessness imbues the whole of civil society. Notions of community, of membership, of belonging and of participation are established here or not at all...The public realm must be reclaimed. Dialogue and inclusion must become political imperatives, and lines of accountability must be clear...There needs to be a new creativity as regards intermediate public institutions, where Britain's constitutional poverty is cruelly exposed."
(Hutton, 1996, pp.286-290).

The language of dialogue, community, participation, accountability, intermediate public institutions, *is* the language social work speaks, even if in recent years it has been largely sequestered within a discourse of quality assurance and consumer satisfaction. Reclaiming 'social space' is also about reclaiming a relationship for child protection work to the public sphere and the language of politics. The example of the Flemish system shows, we believe, that this does not have to entail abandoning a concern for the detail of sensitive interaction with troubled and damaged children and their parents, or the workaday business of the child protection agency. Rather it is a reformulation, and a solidification within society of what these tasks mean.

## Intermediate space in English child protection — where did it go?

When Scottish social workers in our study assembled to view the video of their English colleagues discussing the research case study (see Chapter 3), they began to reflect on the place of the children's panel and the reporter to the panel in their working lives. These workers felt that the panel provided them with a considerable degree of confidence and support in taking risks with families, and in implementing their welfare responsibilities in families with unco-operative parents. One worker contrasted this with her impressions of the English system in which it seemed to her that: "You're immediately thinking about a court stage...". The same practitioner also felt that the panel secures a *welfare orientation* in their work, saying, "There is a punitive element but the whole thing is a welfare system, even at hearings I've very rarely seen a big stick being waved...". Other members introduced a different angle, saying that if parental co-operation is not forthcoming, the panel does make available 'a stick to wave'.

The consensus of the group was that the children's panel introduces a helpful degree of non-punitive authority into a welfare approach. Thus the discussion turned on the social workers' own sense of their relative *empowerment* in response to the case study by comparison with the English group. The group also noted how a range of interested parties to the case could, in principle, make a referral to the reporter — extended family members, day nursery workers, neighbours — and that this embodied both a substantive and symbolic sharing of responsibility for child welfare and protection concerns with other professionals and other citizens. Responsibility for both *care and control* is legally and structurally apportioned so that it rests with a *social* domain, not just a professional one. Thus, the line between citizenship, professional concern and responsibility, and child welfare is drawn not in terms of a division but an inclusion.

The Scottish children's panel constructs 'intermediate space' on different principles to the Flemish mediation committee, straddling the administrative and judicial spheres rather than occupying a position between them. Both in turn differ from the French model and the Francophone Belgian *conseiller*, but all share some common characteristics, one of which is to legitimate the flexible use of different forms of authority in child protection work. Questions of accountability for the power and authority invested in these institutions and roles was a consistent preoccupation of the English workers in our study, but as we suggested that these institutions may embody a conception of welfare more akin to the principle of 'complex fairness' adumbrated by John Gray (1996), than to those of administered social democracy. An equally important, and very contemporary question about such institutions, may arise from a different direction. As Caroline Ball (1996) notes, one source of dissatisfaction with the English juvenile court system which lay behind the reforming impetus of the Children Act was the capacity of a lay magistracy to handle some of the cases which came before the bench. "Care proceedings can be very complex, involving contested medical evidence that is often too

difficult for a lay forum...As a consequence, in the decades prior
to implementation of the Children Act 1989, local authorities
resorted increasingly to the flexible historic common law wardship
jurisdiction of the high court when seeking care orders." (1996,
p.8). Arguably in the crisis which beset Scottish child protection
work in the Orkneys' cases, the capacity of the children's panels to
manage the legal, professional and political complexity of the
situation was sorely tested (Trowell, 1996). Personal relationships
among members of official bodies may compromise the capacity
for justice and objectivity in a deeply divided community dealing
with a highly emotional and controversial investigation. Social
cohesion, community representation, and family conflict may
generate an unmanageable set of tensions in the most complex
cases, suggesting perhaps that an independent 'ombudsman' type
figure is necessary to 'hold the ring' at times within a local child
protection system. The role of the French *inspecteur*, an administrative figure invested with responsibility and powers outside the
judicial sphere may offer a model for this. Our study suggests that
just as locating decision-making power in the hands of judges need
not result in formality and legalism, so also the participation of
'lay' representatives does not guarantee a meaningful connection
to the community. The key determining character of child
protection institutions appears to reside in the extent to which
welfare principles oriented to the needs of complex family
situations inform their conception, whether in the judicial or non-
judicial spheres.

As the crisis surrounding the Dutroux[1] case unfolds in Belgium
and extends to the entire political domain (Helm, 1996), it may be
that the Flemish mediation committee will be exposed in a similar
way to the Orkneys' children's panel. Thus, the discussion which
follows suggesting that negotiative institutions embedded in a
context of political 'localism' represent a way forward in England,
must be tempered by recognition that certain instances of child
abuse and protection, both in here and in a national and
international context, demand institutional responses to match.

Nevertheless, with this caveat in mind, we may reasonably ask
what happened to intermediate space in English child protection
work, and how might it be re-established? We have alluded above
to an earlier phase in the history of English social work when the
professional role was understood to embody an ability to combine
'care and control' in a flexible and specific manner according to the
demands of particular case circumstances. Within this culture,
institutions like the child protection conference could be used to
represent both institutional and symbolic authority, to give a

'message' to families in much the same way that Scottish workers describe above their 'use' of the children's panel. When we examine the surrounding social and political conditions in which this culture was situated, we see that it was not 'protected' or legitimated in the way we have argued the equivalent sphere in the Flemish system to be. We have discussed this point at some length in comparing the English and the French systems, arguing that French paternalism (for all that we may be discomforted by certain aspects of it) is structured into the fabric of social relations, so that any particular encounter between social workers, judges, and citizens is "the concrete embodiment of the paternalistic state with its ties of mutual obligation and duty", whereas, "paternalism in English child care social work turned out to be a contingency." (Cooper, 1995, p.63). Hutton's (1996) analysis of the whole condition of British public and political life turns on much the same point — the absence of *constitutional guarantees* for the freedom of civil society from 'state' interference or control, and the corresponding lack of constitutional support *for these freedoms*. As we show later, in Germany the subsidiarity principle securing the domain of 'civil society' and its competence to expedite affairs free of unnecessary interference is written into the Federal constitution. Thus, in so far as British governments of the last fifteen years have sought to dismantle what they saw as obstacles to 'free market exchange', including the powers invested in local government, trades unions, and other associative institutions in the intermediate sphere between the family and the state, there has been no constitutional protection to hinder or prevent this sweeping programme of socio-economic reform. As Hutton says, "Only one thing is necessary to control the British state; a majority in the House of Commons (1996, p.33). The centralised, nationally regulated and procedurally administered character of the child protection system of England and Wales, could not readily have emerged in any of the continental European states we have studied, because constitutional settlements between the central state and the regions or municipalities do not allow for it. The characteristic predicaments of English child protection work are reflected in many other spheres of public life, and any solutions must take account of the need to secure themselves in the context of a political as well as a professional settlement.

It is often said that Parts III and IV of the Children Act 1989 remain in tension. 'Partnership' is nowhere mentioned in the Act itself, although it crops up frequently in the volumes of accompanying guidance. Perhaps the central argument of this book is that the spirit of the Children Act 1989 is hindered in its realisation by structural conditions in the organisation of British welfare which do not provide a secure and legitimated 'space' (or spaces) in which the very complex set of elements which must be negotiated in partnership practice can be established, worked out over time, renegotiated, refined, researched, and developed. This is what the family group conference model seems to aspire to, but for the moment its strength is confined to representing an alternative to the child protection conference, rather than a contribution to thinking through the principles on which a new social space might be founded. Individual professionals or teams can, and do, successfully improve their practice in the direction of better partnership. But a properly embedded child protection practice culture which enables partnership, requires an institutionally protected environment in which to evolve, and against which to find its agreed limits. This is what England and Wales, and to a lesser extent Scotland, lack. We do not propose that any particular continental model provides an instant answer to English questions. We cannot beg, steal or borrow a new child protection system, but we can learn from others and let them inform our own creative endeavour.

## [1] Public anxiety and child protection in Belgium — a footnote

In a private communication, Liesbet Smeyers, a social worker within the Flemish confidential doctor service makes the following observations in the immediate aftermath of the revelations surrounding the Dutroux affair in September 1996.

"We fear an evolution towards a much more repressive system in cases of sexual abuse. Some people are talking about a duty to report offenders in cases of sexual abuse. This will seriously restrict the possibility of working with offenders, and leaves no room to consider the relationship between the offender and the victim. The victim is pushed aside".

"The confidential doctor service works with all forms of violence to children. In the present atmosphere, the focus is laid on sexual abuse, overlooking other forms such as neglect and emotional abuse. Sexual abuse often occurs together with another form of abuse. The idea is reinforced that sexual abuse has more harmful long-term consequences than other forms of child abuse".

"There is a powerful need for clarity, certainty and control in order to take away fear and create safety. This is contradictory to offering concrete help to children and their families, which confronts us with uncertainty, helplessness, powerlessness and similar feelings. We find that in these concepts there lies a great potential to make contact with a family system".

"Up to now, most of the public reaction concerns proceedings against offenders. Allegations are being made against the judicial system to the effect that it has failed, waited too long to react, and that it has the means to tackle organised paedophilia. There is suspicion that people in powerful positions have blocked the possibility of tackling paedophilia networks and that people are being protected rather than called to account".

# Section Two:
# The Research Process and Findings

This section looks at the research process and findings. In Chapter 3 the complex methodology of the research is described and analysed. Chapter 4 gives a description of the eight different systems of child welfare and child protection that we studied. Chapter 5 analyses some of the differences and similarities between the systems, and points to some of the implications of these differences.

# Chapter 3:
# The methodology of the research

## The initial research questions

When we started our research into European child protection systems and began to look at child protection in France, we had no hypothesis or clear research questions. We did not know whether we would find a system and ways of working that were identical with our own or very different and what the nature of any differences might be. This was no longer the case when we moved on to look at other European countries. We now knew some of the possibilities of difference in other systems. Moreover, what we had already seen in France suggested that it would be impossible that any two systems should be the same; and that the nature of the similarities and differences between two systems and ways of working is enlightening.

When the study was extended, we had a hypothesis that the English system and English practice in child protection would be different from that of the other countries; that these differences would be related to differences in formal structures and cultures; and that there would be some aspects of structures and some aspects of cultures that might be particularly important in determining the nature of practice in child protection. Experience suggested that a deeper understanding of the nature of the English child protection system and practice could be gained from foreign comparisons and that this could be of practical value in enabling change and development in our own system. We had seen one view of English child protection from France. Would the picture we obtained from other countries be the same? If different, in what ways would it be different? Would it reinforce, qualify or contradict the perception of the English system that we had gained from the French comparison?

## The methodology of the research

As far as possible, the same methods were used in this phase of the research as had been used in first phase of the Anglo-French study (Cooper *et al.*, 1992). The aim was twofold; to learn about the child protection system of the other country in terms of how it worked for those directly involved in operating it; and to elicit the views of social workers in one country about the practice and system of another. We therefore wanted to work with practitioners, both to get their help in understanding how their own system worked, and to get their reflections on alternative ways of working as demonstrated in another country. We also needed to work with practitioners in order to understand the systems they worked within. A description of a social work system is almost impossible to understand unless it is attached to case material; equally, it is difficult to get a proper understanding of a social worker's actions and decisions without any knowledge of the surrounding system. The two aspects of understanding had to go forward side by side.

In each country we found a small group of social workers who agreed to meet for two 'seminars' to help us understand their system of child protection in comparison with our own. In England we found a new group to work with each foreign system studied, so that in all we had seven English groups, six drawn from the West London area, one from Humberside.

## The first seminar

At the first seminar, the individual social workers were given a case outline and asked to give written answers to questions on this material. The case was divided into four stages, describing escalating difficulties in a family. The case material was given to them in four stages, and the scope and content of the four questions at each stage were very similar. These were designed to discover what they would do, why they would do it, what the legal constraints and possibilities were, and the theoretical and conceptual basis of their thinking.

After completing individual written answers to the questions, the participants held a loosely structured discussion of the case, starting from a consideration of what they might plan to do at the end point of the development of the case as described. This discussion was videoed, and facilitated by a member of the research team. In the course of this discussion, the researcher had certain prompt questions they could use to further the exploration of the case and ensure that the same range of themes was addressed by every group, but with one exception, these were not much used. The exception was one question which was put to all groups: "Is there anything you might have done differently if this family had been black?" No group raised this issue spontaneously, and it was an area of possible difference that we wanted to explore.

The range of themes we wanted all groups to consider were:

- the plans they might make with the family or its individual members;
- rights and responsibilities of the characters in the study;
- the roles and tasks of professionals, and the differing concerns and preoccupations of system agents represented in groups, including their dilemmas about intervention;
- family and individual dynamics in the case;
- political and social factors which might influence thinking about the case; and
- organisational and institutional factors affecting their response to the case.

These group discussions typically lasted for 40-45 minutes.

## The second seminar

The aim of the second seminar was to discover and record the participants' reactions to the responses of social workers from another country to the identical case study, and parallel case discussion they had undertaken. The participants were first given a brief description of the child protection system in question and of their colleagues' questionnaire responses to the case study. They were shown the video (dubbed into the appropriate language) of their counterparts' group discussion of the case. They were then asked for their reactions to what they had heard about the other country — what had they found different, similar, striking, or puzzling — and their reflections on their own system and practice in the light of what they had heard about the other. This discussion was also video recorded, and facilitated by a researcher.

## The case study

The case was a fictional situation, created jointly by French and English researchers to illustrate some common problems that face social workers in both countries. It was constructed to be as far as possible free of specific national organisational landmarks, and this limited the amount of information that could be given, especially in terms of any judicial involvement, since systems and practices diverge so widely in this respect. The case involved a three generation family. In the English text (the names were altered according to the country) there was a grandmother, Mrs Smith, who was concerned about her daughter, Valerie, who was married to Jack, and there were problems in the marriage. Valerie had a 13 year old daughter, Frances who was the child of a previous relationship, and a four year old son, Andrew. The narrative concerns a series of referrals centred on the children: Andrew is reported by his playgroup to be violent, Frances briefly runs away from home, and hints at problems with her step-father. The parents, Valerie and Jack, reject offers of help and do not wish the social workers to be involved; only Frances keeps up a contact with the social worker, but says no more about her relationship with her step-father. The same case outline and the same questions were used in all countries.

## CASE STUDY

**Stage one**

Mrs Smith contacts the social services department. She says that she is worried about her daughter's marital problems. She is not specific about the nature of the marital problems. She also conveys anxieties about the nature of the relationship between her son-in-law and her granddaughter, her daughter's child by a previous marriage. Her daughter's family comprises:

| | | |
|---|---|---|
| Father: | Jack | age 40 |
| Mother: | Val | age 33 (Mrs Smith's Daughter) |
| Daughter: | Frances | age 13 (Mrs Smith's granddaughter, Jack's step-daughter) |
| Son: | Andrew | age 4 (Mrs Smith's grandson) |

The family is not known to the social services department.

**Stage two**

Valerie and Jack have refused to see the social worker so there is no further contact until one month later, when the worker at the playgroup attended by Andrew contacts the social services department because she is concerned about him. She says that his attendance at the playgroup is irregular, that he is excessively violent towards the other children and that his mother seems depressed.

**Stage three**

Two weeks later, the social worker has seen Valerie once, but did not get much information from her. Frances' teacher contacts the social services department. Frances has asked her teacher if she can talk with a social worker. She has run away from home for three days and has just returned. She complains of violence between her parents. She also expresses a concern that her relationship with her step-father is more intimate than she would like it to be, but she will not say more about it.

**Stage four**

In the course of discussions with the social worker, Frances decides that she wishes to stay at home but that she wishes to continue to have help from the social worker. Eight days later, the playgroup worker contacts the social services department again. She says that Andrew is increasingly violent and distressed. The worker has suggested that Valerie should take him to the doctor but she has refused. The worker is worried about Andrew. Frances says that the marital violence is continuing, but that her mother does not wish to leave home. Frances says no more about her relationship with her step-father.

## Analysing the data

The data arising from the process described yielded information on a number of inter-related levels. This was analysed using content and thematic analysis.

Material in Seminar 1 yielded information on:

- practice thinking and behaviour, and its theoretical under-pinnings;
- opportunities and constraints on the use of resources including the law;
- conceptualisations of the family, the place of children within the family, and their relationship to social authority and the state;
- conceptualisations of need, risk, abuse, protection, normal and deviant behaviour; and
- criteria for decision-making, including dilemmas and predicaments.

Material in Seminar 2, further elucidated the above and developed, through the experience of 'difference', new perspectives in relation to:

- observations about the other country's practice behaviours, concepts, predicaments, and 'silences' when compared to the 'home' response;
- observations about practitioners' own 'home' responses to the case, thrown into relief by the differences experienced in the other country. 'Silences' are now discovered in the home context, when experienced in relation to the comparative 'noise' made by the other country;
- interpretations about why the home situation is like it is, and what values, philosophies, or principles explain or account for it; and
- interpretations, or more often questions and puzzles, about why the foreign situation is like it is.

Typical examples of the above were:

"I noticed they spent much more time actually discussing the family and trying to understand what was happening inside it, than we did. We spent much more time discussing procedures."

"I was surprised that they thought they could interview Frances without the consent of the parents. They seem not to think about the rights of parents, on the other hand I can see it would be really helpful to have the freedom to do what they did."

"They seemed to have confidence in the judge. It's hard to

imagine having a relationship like that with an English magistrate. It makes me wonder what kind of figure a judge is in Germany."

**Figure 1**

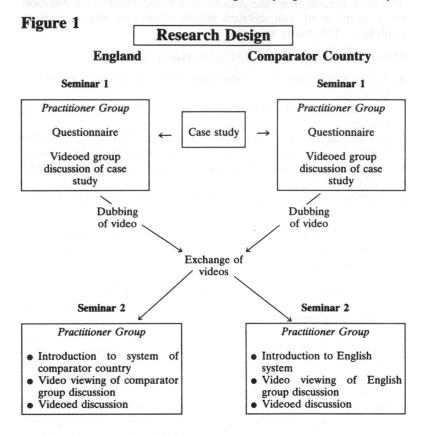

## The interpretive link

Throughout the study, the research team was gathering information and understanding about the characteristics of each of the systems. Some of this was relatively 'hard' data such as information about legislation and organisational structures, some of it 'softer' such as material about the culture of the family in a particular country, or the education and training of practitioners. What we strove for in relation to each country studied was a *plausible interpretation of the data gathered from the research groups, in the light of the characteristics of the child protection system as we now understood it.*

Above all, we concluded that it is impossible to give a

single, accurate, final account of 'a child protection system', not because of lack of information, but because all aspects of 'a system' are in the end social constructions produced by a complex interaction among those who are involved with it, including families. All these actors or groups of actors, explicitly or more often implicitly bring their own interpretations to bear on their own or each others' behaviour all the time. The stable and characteristic patterns of behaviour and meaning which are what allow us to make statements such as: 'Child protection in England is like this and in Italy is like that', are simply the product of implicit or explicit consensus about values, behaviour, constraints on behaviour, and the criteria for decision-making. It is tempting to point to entities such as 'the law' or 'the structure of the system' and say that these are not matters of interpretation, but fact. Our position is that they *approach* the status of 'fact' more closely than some other features of a system, but only by virtue of being comparatively stable, well-legitimated features of the system, which operate as constraining and enabling factors on behaviour only so as long as they are legitimated, or people continue to give their consent to them.

## Figure 2

| Structure of data gathering and analysis |
| --- |

| England | Comparator Country |
| --- | --- |
| Data from English group about own system | Data from comparator group about own system |
| Group's interpretations of Comparator system | Group's interpretations of English system |
| Group's reflexive understanding of own system | Group's reflexive understanding of own system |
| Content and theme analysis | Content and theme analysis |

> Comparative study, using group's self interpretations, and interpretations of other system, linked to researcher's knowledge of system characteristics to produce accounts of relationships between practice behaviour and thinking, and system characteristics.

| English System Description Structure, culture, organisation | Comparator System Description Structure, culture, organisation |
| --- | --- |
| Seven English Groups | —— Global comparison between England and seven other systems | —— Seven Comparator Country Groups |

The force of this way of looking at things can be appreciated in England in the wake of the implementation of the Children Act 1989, following which there continues to be a widespread professional debate about what it means in whole or in part. The move away from 'child protection' towards 'family support' involves assigning new meanings to and deconstructing old ones about Section 47 of the Act. The Children Act 1989 did not prescribe these meanings, and the present period of professional uncertainty about the 'meaning' of all sorts of central concepts — 'protection', 'support', and 'need' — is a sign of a system in the process of change, and as concepts and meanings mutate, so it is actually hard for people to know how to act professionally. Certain features of the English system remain comparatively stable at present, but interestingly certain aspects of it would be very hard for a researcher to describe accurately at this time, because consenses and legitimation have been disturbed in pursuit of new ways of thinking and acting.

## The countries chosen

We were limited by resources in the number of countries we could work with, and this affected our choice of countries. We wanted one country from southern Europe, and chose Italy rather than other Mediterranean countries because of existing contacts there. It seemed important to take the research to Germany because of its significance within the EU, and its size. We wanted to include Belgium and the Netherlands because their proximity made them potentially more likely to have systems near to our own and also because they both had versions of a 'confidential doctor' service. We wanted to include Scotland because they have a different legal system operating within the same national structures. It is a matter of regret that there are many countries we were not able to include, in particular the Scandinavian countries.

## The limitations and the possibilities of the methodology

The case study and discussion material described above was supported by information about the child protection systems drawn from a variety of oral and written sources, including researchers and practitioners in all countries. However, there are many gaps in information and understanding in relation to all the countries that we studied, notwithstanding the perspective advanced above of the impossibility of arriving at a 'final' account. We would therefore emphasise that all this work is provisional, and only begins to develop an understanding of each of the other systems. While there is no intention to mislead, misinterpret, or offer tendentious accounts of any system, we hope that if these are present they will lead to constructive refutation, and alternative interpretations. This is how knowledge advances.

Quite apart from these limitations in background knowledge, there are limitations to the use we can make of the information gathered. In each country we are relying on the reactions of a small group of social workers. There is no way that we can regard them as reliably representative of their peers. They are however, potentially representative of their peers. This was checked to some extent in the Anglo-French phase of the research, when we recruited two groups in each country to check whether we might be getting very idiosyncratic responses. This did not appear to be a problem; the groups in each country producing very similar material. In England where we have worked over time with a larger number of groups, the reactions to the case have been consistent, only showing some change of emphasis after the implementation of the Children Act 1989 and the subsequent development of child protection procedures.

This is not the only cross-national research in the social work field to use a 'vignette' technique to compare practice in different countries, although as far as we know it is the only study to use reflexive feedback from one country to another as part of the research. Soydan and Stal (1994) used the vignette technique on a larger scale in a comparative study of social work responses to a child abuse case with English and Swedish social workers. Even with a much greater number of participants there were problems in making generalisations from the participants' responses; we have to emphasise that we do not seek to make generalisations about 'what Belgian (or German or etc) social workers think' or 'what English social workers think (or do)'. What we have is a series of pictures. These pictures show us how a certain set of events might be handled in different countries, and what the thinking behind the action would be; they show us that picture and they show us a reflection of that picture through the eyes of a group of social workers in another country. They show us English child protection practice reflected in seven different mirrors all held at different angles.

This research is exploratory and descriptive, but also inter-pretive. Within the descriptions, certain themes appear and reappear as the social workers looked at differences and similar-ities between their different reactions to the case. The themes emerge where there is a coincidence in the reaction of workers from several different countries to the English system, or of several English groups to different foreign systems. Although we only have a fragment from each country, the fragments appear to be part of the same map.

## The potential value of the study

We consider that the data from this research is useful for raising questions in ways that make new answers possible. Debates about the efficacy of a system, and about possible change, tend to take place within a narrow frame of reference, largely set by the existing system. Thus at the point where the 'reflexivity' of the research participants comes in to play, as they become aware of the previously unrecognised assumptions and limits of their own way of thinking and working, they can be thought of as making the transition from normal to revolutionary science in Kuhn's terms (see Chapter 1). They are now examining the limits and defining features of the paradigm within which they work. We want to draw out certain features of the methodology to articulate a tentative thesis about the relationship between research, practice, and policy, which combines with the work of the social theorists discussed in Chapter 1 as relevant to thinking about the present state of English child protection work.

We have made the point that in this process, we as researchers underwent a series of changes which led us to see our own system and practices differently. It is an integral aspect of the approach that the research relies on practitioners' *experience* for its primary data. People who operate the systems, who actively produce and reproduce them day by day, are thus themselves exposed to the process of change described and potentially led to re-evaluate their own practice accordingly, and to see possibilities for change in an organic fashion.

As a result, the distinction between the researcher and the researched is largely dissolved. It is the capacity for *reflexivity* — the ability of practitioners to research their own conditions of social life and their own activity as producers of meaning — which allows this dissolution. Researchers occupy a meta-position, recording and synthesising the data produced by practitioners, and linking it to their own reflexive productions.

Thus, in disseminating this work, we have been led increasingly to attempt to reproduce with others (in necessarily condensed forms) the experiences we have ourselves been through. We have done this in the form of quasi-experiential events in which groups are exposed to first hand accounts of foreign practice, and we hope then led to think creatively about possibilities for change within the English system. One of these is reported in Cooper *et al.*, (1997) *Can Europe Show us a Third Way?*

In summary, this is a concept of research *as* intervention, *as* policy change, rather than research as transmission or as an aid to the technical fix for a malfunctioning machine. If the research *aims* to produce change, then this must be set against the recognition that stability is also a condition which is actively produced by the human agents who constitute systems.

The view advanced above of research and social life as the productions of reflexively aware actors who create meanings relies heavily on the work of the British social theorist Anthony Giddens. Within a diverse range of preoccupations Giddens' work is notable for having tried to resolve the traditional sociological dichotomy of social structure and human agency. This polarity has bedevilled the history of social work theory and education in Britain, tending to encourage spurious allegiences either to a 'deterministic' left inclined social theory emphasising social structure as a constraining force which produces or accounts for social inequality, or to voluntaristic and psychologically oriented theory which stresses the freedom and capacity for change in individuals. For Giddens, the concept of reflexivity is a bridge across this divide, since social structure is seen not on the model of the fixed framework of a building, but as the product of recurring patterns of meaning and behaviour belonging to self-aware social actors who are knowledgeable about the constraints and opportunities of the social life they help to produce and reproduce.

Further, reflexivity is an expanding phenomena: ordinary people are becoming more and more knowledgeable about social life, and as a consequence more and more questioning about previously taken for granted aspects of their conditions of life such as relations with experts and professionals. The social authority which professionals, including social workers, once relied on for their mandate is now a matter which they may have to justify, negotiate, or enter into dialogue about. It cannot be taken for granted. One of the ways in which this occurs is through sociological understanding becoming absorbed back into society itself — what was the 'object of study' now incorporates the study of itself into its own way of life and changes as a consequence. This *double hermeneutic*, as Giddens terms it, is remarkably similar to the process described above at the heart of the methodology of our study. There, in observing and studying another child protection system, practitioners become aware of the underlying principles informing their own behaviour, and may incorporate this back into a changed understanding of themselves and changed behaviour.

As we noted in Chapter 1, Giddens and others take the view that the whole political domain in modern societies must now take account of reflexivity. Lifestyle politics, identity politics, and the 'new social movements' represent not just a diversification of traditional forms of political life, but a challenge to them. Constant and enlarged awareness of the range of 'differences' in the world, means that one's own way of life cannot be seen as 'natural', 'normal' or 'traditional' any more, but just one among a range of possible ways to live. It starts to fall within the category of a choice, rather than an inevitability. This leads to a decline in social passivity, and a disaffection with forms of politics which treat populations as the object of control. People may appear to be more indifferent to the political process, but this is counter-balanced by a politicisation of more everyday concerns. Giddens (1994) cites the enormous growth of self-help groups as one instance of this development. Certainly in his view, traditional representative democracy cannot deliver the forms of active engagement in the political process which the modern, reflexively aware citizen expects. This leads him to promote his ideas of deliberative, dialogic, and negotiative political processes. Arguably, this analysis can be extended to make sense of the whole project of cross-national comparative research, if it is understood as generating a dialogue between 'cultures' previously ignorant of one another in particular respects. Thus the research both flows from and contributes to the process of 'globalisation' or 'Europeanisation' which produces the conditions of life associated with 'reflexive modernity'. These points are explored more fully in Cooper (1995).

Thus we would argue, that the methodology of the research programme *models* something important about the demands of contemporary social life. It begins from the assumption that practitioners are *knowledgeable about the conditions of their own social (work) activity*, and that in entering into a process of research as changed or expanded awareness, 'truth' is being actively created rather than 'discovered'. The mistake (methodological and political) of positivist social research, alluded to in the introduction of this book, is to treat social life as a passive object of study. The stance we promote is not quite the same as a traditional 'user research' perspective, although it shares some of the same values and aims. Our approach aims to avoid polarising and binary conceptions of power and powerlessness, in favour of a recognition that relations and dynamics of power are multiple and shifting. The 'openness to difference' which the methodology encourages and relies upon leads, at its best, to the kind of disturbance of taken for granted assumptions about professional activity provoked by genuine openness to the influence of clients' and users' own knowledgeability about their lives. But just as we have had to combat the tendency to idealise or deride aspects of the English system, and those of other countries, so we think it unhelpful to see 'participation', or user and practitioner involvement in research, as a total relinquishment of power by professionals. Nigel Parton (1996), reviewing *Messages from Research* notes how little the summary has to say about the activity of social work itself. We hope that our study goes some small way to rectifying this omission, mainly through its effort to treat seriously the knowledgeability of social workers in all countries.

# Chapter 4:
# The eight systems of child protection

## Introduction

This chapter sets out descriptions of the eight systems in a framework that allows for comparison between them. The descriptions are not detailed, but aim to give the essential elements. The degree and nature of difference between the systems means that detailed comparisons get extremely complicated; it seemed more useful to use a common framework to give a broader picture, which would enable the reader to make their own comparisons.

The system descriptions are not necessarily intended to be read straight through. They are equally for reference. They do not contain all the details which may be referred to elsewhere in the book. They are outline maps rather than street plans.

## The Framework

The framework we have used needs some explanation.

**Getting Help** describes the entry to the system. If you are a family needing help (in your own view or someone else's), how do you set about getting help? What door do you knock on, whose office do you telephone? Who may knock on your door, who employs the person you engage with?

The **Administrative System** describes the way in which governmental and non-governmental agencies divide the task involved. The use of the term 'administrative' in this context has been borrowed from France; it covers the area sometimes described in England as non-statutory. It includes the work of non-governmental organisations which play differing roles in different systems, but whose role is always important. The administrative system includes the organisation of social services for children and families and the co-operation with other agencies as set up in the UK by *Working Together under the Children Act 1989* (1991).

The **Grounds for Intervention** include both the grounds on which help might be offered (for example, the Children Act 1989 definition of a 'child in need'), and the grounds for legal intervention and the use of compulsion.

The **Legal System** looks very briefly at salient aspects of the law and the courts in relation to child welfare and the powers of the judge.

The **Interface with the Legal System** describes the ways in which systems deal with the area in which their administrative and legal systems meet.

## Translations and meanings

Where we have kept foreign words they are italicised. We have not translated words which we think are easily identifiable (such as the French *assistant social* for social worker) or where the word is nearly the same as in English, but the difference needs to be made clear (such as *audience*, the court hearing of the French judge for children). We have translated almost all terms from Dutch, Flemish and Italian, as being less likely to be familiar to English readers. We have kept some German terms (e.g. *Jugendamt* for youth office) as this may make it easier for the reader to distinguish the German system from the Dutch and the Flemish; many of the official titles when translated are quite similar, which becomes confusing. For example the youth assistance service in the Netherlands is very different from the German youth office (*Jugendamt*).

In the glossary we give the terms and names used throughout the book, cross-referenced where both foreign and English versions have been used, and giving a brief definition. In addition, we draw the reader's attention below to certain words which have different or wider meanings but cannot easily be translated without using a misleading English equivalent.

**Education:** the similar French word *éducation* implies a very much wider concept which includes all aspects of a child's upbringing, social, emotional and intellectual. Related to this is the concept of **pedagogy**, which does not have the negative overtones which the English word holds. Pedagogy refers to knowledge and understanding of how children learn and develop in all aspects of their life, and reflects a similar concept of child development to *éducation*. Social pedagogy is about work with children in their total life experience, and is a holistic concept. **Therapy** is a word used more widely by English social workers; it covers a great deal that would be called *éducation* or pedagogy elsewhere. The continental use of therapy refers to medically-based interventions, whether physical or psychiatric, and the word psychiatric is less avoided.

**Youth:** the word in German, Flemish and Dutch which appears very obviously to translate as 'youth' in English is more inclusive in those languages. German legislation and organisational names refer to *Jugend*, but this does not exclude children. Similarly, the Flemish committee for special youth assistance includes children. On the other hand, the youth assistance service in the Netherlands works with young people from 12 to 25. Youth therefore can cover a very wide age range.

**Committee:** this seems to be used rather more widely than in English, and the service run by a committee is sometimes referred to as the 'committee' rather than as the 'service', e.g. the Flemish special youth assistance service is sometimes referred to as the committee for special youth assistance. There also seems to be some uncertainty as to the translation of 'committee', and the mediation committee is in some places referred to as the mediation commission.

## BELGIUM — THE FLEMISH COMMUNITY

### Getting help

In accordance with the principle of subsidiarity, there is an extensive network of voluntary agency provisions at a local level. These offer a wide range of services and approaches, counselling services, family centres, advice centres of various kinds and general social work support services. There is also a generic local social service run by the commune (the most local unit of local government). A family could go to any of these services, but could alternatively choose to go directly to a service dealing with more difficult or serious childcare problems.

The local services, whether voluntary or commune run, can provide a range of practical help and varying levels of psychological help. They can also refer families to more specialist services such as the equivalent of a child and family guidance clinic. If a worker at this level feels that there are more serious or complex problems than can be worked with in her agency, she can refer the family to the official specialist service for children and families, the service of the committee for special youth assistance, or to one of the confidential doctor centres.

## The administrative system

The voluntary agencies are the major providers of a range of social work services. They work with the statutory agencies at all levels. They provide most residential care and run fostering services. Their funding comes partly from charitable donations and the churches (if they are religious organisations) and partly from local or central government contracts or fees.

The best known of the specialist voluntary agencies is *Kind in Nood*, which runs confidential doctor centres. These centres (there are four in the Flemish community and Brussels) offer a service to families in difficulty which is on a voluntary basis. They will accept and follow up referrals from other agencies and from individuals, while preserving their anonimity, but will only intervene with the agreement of the parents and children. It is not impossible for referral to be made to the legal system but it is very unusual.

The specialist service for children and families is run by the committee for special youth assistance. There is a committee in each administrative district consisting of 12 members appointed by the Flemish government. They are selected from members of youth organisations or youth services, at least one third must be under 30, and in any region where more than 5% of the population are 'migrants', at least one member must have relevant special knowledge. Each committee is operationalised by a bureau for special youth assistance which runs a service for individuals and families, the service of special youth assistance.

There is also a juvenile court social service for the Flemish community, which works with children and young people who are on court orders.

## The grounds for intervention

The mandate for the special youth assistance service is to give help where there is a 'problematic educational (upbringing) situation'. In the legislation that established the service in 1990, there was a change from 'youth protection' (under the 1965 law) to 'youth assistance' and the concept of 'the child in danger' was changed to the 'problematic educational situation'. The aim was to strengthen work on a voluntary basis and to prevent referral into the legal system. The SYA service works with families to co-ordinate and ensure the provision of services by themselves or other agencies. They work on a voluntary basis and cannot work without the agreement of the family. Children of 14 and over have to give their agreement individually. The grounds for referral to the law are that there is a 'problematic educational situation', that cannot be resolved on a voluntary basis, in which the child's emotional, moral, intellectual or social development is in danger (Pieck undated).

## The legal system

The legal system is inquisitorial. The same system covers child protection and juvenile justice, and the grounds for intervention imply a welfare rather than a rights basis. The court system is relatively informal. The judges for children are qualified judges without specialised training.

The powers of the judge for children include the ability to make a range of orders:

- A supervision order under the Flemish community social service to the juvenile court.
- Compulsory family counselling (up to one year).
- Compulsory 'educational' project for the child and if appropriate parent/s.
- Placement in a 'semi-residential' centre (i.e. day care).
- Placement in a reception or orientation centre (maximum 30 days).
- Placement in an observation centre (maximum 60 days).
- Foster care placement (if under 12, up to the age of 13; if 12 or over, for no longer than one year, extendable by one year).
- Residential placement in an open institution (maximum one year).
- Residential placement in a closed institution (maximum 63 months).

The emergency powers of the public prosecutor come into force when there is an urgent need for help, assistance on a voluntary basis is impossible and the 'integrity' of the child is in danger. In this situation, the mediation committee is by-passed, and provisional orders lasting 45 days can be made.

## The interface with the legal system

If the SYA service and the family do not agree, or the objectives of the intervention are not met, the matter is taken to the mediation committee. The mediation committees (one in each judicial district) are set up by the Flemish government, who appoint six members to each committee. Their task is to meet with the family and social workers where either the help proposed is refused by parent/s or child, or where the family has been refused help. Referral to the mediation committee can be from the child, the parents, recognised helping services, the SYA bureau or the judge for children (via the public prosecutor). The mediation committee has no judicial role. They have to attempt to mediate an agreement between the child, parents and services, so that work can continue. If an agreement cannot be reached, the mediation committee can refer the case via the public prosecutor to the judge for children. Unresolved cases do not have to be referred into the legal system. As (except in emergencies) only the mediation committee can refer cases to the legal system, it has considerable power and responsibility. However, the public prosecutor has the final decision as to whether there are legal grounds for referral.


# BELGIUM — THE FRANCOPHONE COMMUNITY

## Getting help

In acordance with the principle of subsidiarity, there is an extensive network of non-governmental agency provision of services at a local level. These offer a wide range of services and approaches, counselling services, family centres, advice centres of various kinds and general social work support services. There is also a generic local social service run by the commune (the most local unit of local government). A family could go to any of these services, but could alternatively choose to go directly to a service dealing with more difficult or serious child care problems.

The local services, whether non-governmental or commune run, can provide a range of practical help and varying levels of psychological help. They can also refer families to more specialist services such as the equivalent of a child and family guidance clinic. If a worker at this level feels that there are more serious or complex problems than can be worked with in her agency, she can refer the family to the official specialist service for children and families, *Service de l'Aide à la Jeunesse* (see below), or to *SOS Enfance*, which provides a confidential service for families in difficulties similar to the Flemish confidential doctor service of *Kind in Nood*.

## The administrative system

The non-governmental agencies are the major providers of a range
of social work services. They work with the statutory agencies at
all levels. They provide most residential care and run fostering
services. Their funding comes partly from charitable donations
and the churches (if they are religious organisations) and partly
from local or central government contracts or fees.

*SOS Enfance* is a non-governmental organisation with state
funding which works with families in difficulties. It provides a
confidential and voluntary service and takes referrals from
children, parents, relatives, members of the public and from other
social service agencies. It is expected that it will be possible to
work on a voluntary basis, and in most cases this happens. It is
possible to refer a case into the formal system if a child is
considered to be in danger.

The specialist service for children and families is the *Conseil de
l'Administration de l'Aide à la Jeunesse* (CAAJ), which is funded
and administered at the community level. There is a CAAJ in each
judicial district, providing for preventive work on a general level
and for a social work service for individual families and children,
the *Service de l'Aide à la Jeunesse* (SAJ). The overall head of the
service is the director, who is responsible for the organisation and
administration of social services for children and families. He is a
member of the CAAJ and is appointed by the government.

The head of the SAJ is the *conseiller* (adviser), appointed by the
government, often a trained lawyer. Cases are referred to the SAJ
when there are problems in achieving a satisfactory outcome
through other agencies. The *conseiller* can either refer the case
back to the services of the commune (basic generic social services
and community health services), or see the family and the social
worker concerned and work out a contract with the family. The
contract that the *conseiller* makes can be for placement or for work
with the child and family in the community. The term *action
éducatif au milieu ouvert* is used. As in France it implies a package
of social work help to child and family that aims to improve
parenting and social skills through a variety of means. If the child
is 14 or over, s/he has to sign the contract as well as the parents.
The contract is a negotiated programme of aid.

There is also a court social work service, the *Service de
Protection Judiciaire*, which provides a social work service for the
judge for children. This service undertakes work in juvenile justice
cases (*protection judiciare*).

## The grounds for intervention

The services provided by non-governmental agencies are provided according to the aims, objectives and policies of the individual organisations. The SAJ provides *aide sociale* for children who are defined as being 'in difficulty' or 'in danger', on the basis that children and their families have a right to specialist and professional help.

Referral to the legal system takes place when the physical or mental and emotional integrity (well-being) of a child is seriously and currently endangered and there has been a failure to reach a voluntary agreement (Lebrun, 1992).

## The legal system

The legal system is inquisitorial. The same system covers child protection and juvenile justice, and the grounds for intervention imply a welfare rather than a rights basis. The court system is relatively informal. The judges for children are qualified judges without specialised training.

The powers of the judge for children include the ability to make a range of orders including supervision and for residential or foster care. The orders are not time limited, but should be reviewed annually. Social work on judicial orders in child protection is carried out by the SAJ.

## The interface with the legal system

Since the legislation of 1991, the aim has been to prevent children from entering the legal process. The SAJ works on this basis and the role of the *conseiller* is to deflect cases from referral into the judicial system by providing a place for dialogue and negotiation between the family and the social worker. The *conseiller* cannot take any compulsory action. If agreement cannot be reached, and the child is at risk, he has to refer the case to the children's judge. The *conseiller* has to record in writing the reasons for his decisions as to what help to offer. If agreement cannot be reached both the *conseiller* and the family have the right to refer the case to the children's judge, who will review the correctness of the *conseiller's* plan, and, if necessary, make an order. The judge can send a case back to the *conseiller*. In an emergency, a referral can be made direct to the office of the public prosecutor, who is responsible for all referrals to the judge for children, and who has the power to intervene and take police action if necessary.

## FRANCE

### Getting help

A family approaching the system is almost certain to make their first approach to the *assistant social de secteur* (AS). This is the gencric social worker who is employed by the departmental social services in the area team. The AS has a specific patch, and is responsible for the population of the patch. This responsibility continues even if the family is being seen by other specialist workers. The equivalent of the health visitor works in the same area team as the social workers, so referral is frequent and easy from community health to social work. The departmental service provides family aides and specialist children and family social workers. They can also make referrals to the child guidance services. There is a telephone referral system, the *ligne vert*, open to adults and children.

### The administrative system

The main framework of the administrative system is provided by the departmental social service and its specialist section, *Aide Sociale à l'Enfance* (ASE). The AS of the area team provides the generic service; if she considers more help is needed, she can ask for further work to be undertaken by ASE. The *inspecteur* of ASE decides in consultation with the area team, what level and nature of resources should be offered, and negotiates this with the parents. A formal package called an AEMO, *Assistance Éducative en Milieu Ouvert*, may be negotiated. This is a time limited package of help which might involve counselling, practical help and intensive work with children or parents. All these actions depend on the voluntary agreement of the family. Work with the families of children in care is done either by the AS or by a social worker attached to the residential or fostering institution in question.

Voluntary agencies have an important role, but they are not usually the first point of contact. They provide some of the residential and fostering services used by the departmental social services. Under contract to the social services department, they provide prevention teams (on a community and youth work model) and specialist teams to work with children and families on an AEMO. They do most of the work on judicial AEMOs and do assessments for the judge for children.

There are social work services provided by the Ministry of

Justice which also provide an assessment service for the children's judge and work with some children on AEMOs.

## The grounds for intervention

The departmental social services are readily available to families seeking help. There are no specific grounds such as being 'in need' that define whether or not a child is eligible for help.

The grounds for legal intervention are that the conditions for a child's upbringing are being seriously endangered and that there is no effective co-operation from the parents.

## The legal system

The legal system is inquisitorial and welfare based. There is no separation between child protection and juvenile justice, though the attitude of the judge may differ, and different social work services might be preferred. The process of the hearings is informal and the family is in direct discussion with the judge. The training for children's judges is the same as for all judges, and a post as judge for children is a normal part of a judge's career pattern.

The main judicial orders are:

- Assessment (usually a three month order).
- Supervision orders (AEMO).
- Placement orders (either residential or foster care).

The judge has wide discretionary powers, and can intervene in the process of a case. By law, the judge has to attempt to get the agreement of the parents to any order he makes, and failure to do this can be grounds for an appeal. However, the judge can determine the level of parental contact, and can over-rule the parents on such things as the choice of residential or foster care. Orders are time limited, and have to be reviewed at least every two years. The same judge stays with a case throughout, and so may get to know the family quite well. The judge cannot sever all connection between child and parents or authorise an adoption.

In an emergency, referral is made to the public prosecutor who can take immediate action using the police.

## The interface with the legal system

Referrals from the social services department have to be agreed with the *inspecteur* of ASE, who would expect to attempt to achieve a voluntary agreement with the parents. If this failed, referral would be via the public prosecutor to the judge for children. The social services department is not the only means of referral to the judge; other institutions such as hospitals can refer, and so can the parents or the child, and other close relatives.

The *inspecteur* has an important role in providing a negotiating space before referral to the judicial system, but the judicial system is quite readily used. Referral to the legal system takes place readily, and parents as well as social workers use the possibility of recourse to the judge for children, either in their dealings with social workers, or in relation to disputes within the wider family. Judicial supervision orders (AEMOs) are common, and their extension is often requested by parents. Cases come to the French judge for children more readily than in the other systems that we studied, and more negotiation takes place with the judge. The period of a three month assessment order (an order that is frequently made at the outset), can be used for an exploration of possibilities and the judge sometimes is involved in the brokerage of arrangements within the family that might take place outside the judicial sphere in other systems. Assessment is separate from investigation. Investigation is undertaken by the police at the request of the judge.

## GERMANY

### Getting help

Germany is a federal state whose individual states or *Länder* have considerable autonomy over the implementation of federally decreed legislation relating to children and families. The ways of getting help depend on regionally and locally developed services which are offered by primarily voluntary or private organisations but often with the financial support of the local authority and the youth office or *Jugendamt* in a monitoring role.

Families looking for help might approach the local voluntary organisation most closely tailored to their requirements, a neighbourhood centre, for instance, run by the large national charity *Caritas* or the *Diakonische Werk*, which is the protestant charity. They could approach the youth service directly and might be referred on to a range of broadly educational, remedial or therapeutic services in the voluntary sector. They could be offered help from one of their own services, such as intensive long-term family support on contract, the health service might provide diagnostic assessment for children with emotional difficulties, and in-patient treatment in special units and centres. Children themselves can ask for services and can receive confidential counselling in their own right but only if the aim of counselling would be undermined if their parents or legal guardians were told.

In cases of child or young person abuse, specialist agencies, like the *Kinderschutzdienst* or child protection service, offer a local helpline, confidential counselling and family therapy but not necessarily in every town or district. A local directory lists available services yet it can still be confusing to know which to choose. In the new federal states some of the specialist organisations are not yet established but new initiatives are constantly being developed in line with the principle of subsidiarity which means that services provided by locally-based voluntary groups are encouraged in favour of those initiated by local government.

## The administrative system

The main responsibility for statutory work is vested in the youth office at town, district and regional level. The youth office combines a range of services for families and children which includes youth care in the wider sense of recreational and pastoral provisions, responsibilities towards single parents including the administration of child support payments, fostering and adoption, and a social work service which is usually organised on a patch basis but can also take other organisational forms. The youth office and the youth services committee in every administrative district are responsible for the development and support of all the preventive services initiated in recent child care legislation and have to do this by co-ordinating and monitoring private and voluntary organisations within their area. One provision introduced by the *Kinderjugendhilfegesetz* 1990 (Child and Youth Service Act) is universal nursery provisions for all children over three, to be implemented over a period of six years. The youth service committee has representatives from the community and from voluntary organisations on its board, as well as representatives from health, education, minority interest groups, the Church, and, of course, the youth office.

Voluntary agencies are by far the main providers of child care services, such as day care, foster care and residential accommodation which are seen as an extension of family care. The endeavour to rehabilitate or at least maintain contact with the natural family is paramount. Voluntary and statutory agencies aim to implement the spirit of the child care act to work in partnership with parents and to support children in their families. Where several agencies are involved or complex decisions need to be taken the so-called educational conference or helpers' meeting is called and parents are invited to attend as are young people if they wish to be present.

## Grounds for intervention

According to the most recent child care legislation the youth office has a statutory duty to support the family in the task of caring for, and educating children and helping them to grow into self-reliant and responsible citizens. Whilst parents have the responsibility to carry out this task, the youth office, as agents of the state, have a duty to ensure that parents are sufficiently enabled and supported. Children who are not protected or are in need of help may require the additional powers of the guardianship or family courts to receive appropriate help and protection. In cases of emergencies, children can be removed without an order but with the judge's knowledge and agreement. In those cases parents or caretakers need to be informed immediately and heard within a day. Provisional orders in respect of parental responsibility for the health or the education of a child or children can be made and may need a hearing before they are confirmed if there is disagreement. Children themselves can ask to be taken to a safe place against their parents wishes which can be arranged at short notice. Either side can subsequently apply for a variation of the order.

Parents and children are eligible for representation in civil court proceedings although children are generally represented by their social worker, who may come from a voluntary agency. If children have guardians as a result of previous court intervention, their guardian, who may be a private individual, an organisation or the youth office, will represent them.

## The legal system

The Federal Government sets the framework for legislation and the structure for the judiciary. Individual *Länder* have their own legislative and executive powers and will implement the legislation according to their requirements but with the directives given by the Federal Government. The Child and Youth Services Act of 1990 is the most recent piece of legislation to combine previous acts and to introduce extensive preventive and supportive measures to help with the care and education of children in their families. Other legislation and the Federal constitution set out parental powers and responsibilities and the child's right to care and education. Criminal matters are decided in separate youth courts which have also a welfare function and are advised by the youth service as to suitable provision, again often along educational lines. The age of criminal responsibility is 14.

The family and guardianship courts operate on the principle of 'voluntary jurisdiction' which provides the legal framework for an inquisitorial system, where parties can be represented and witnesses can be heard; but grounds for an order do not have to be proved in adversarial proceedings before an order is made. The professionally trained judges aim to discuss matters with all interested parties in their offices rather than in formal hearings and efforts are made that parents and children see the same judge. Judges in the guardianship and family courts can make orders to:

- remove and restore some or all parental responsibilities for bringing up children;
- regulate contact;
- order a range of preventive services, including intensive and highly trained specialist help in the home to prevent family break-up;
- provide specialist provision for children with special needs, including emotional needs;
- provide specialist educational help including placement away from home;
- appoint a guardian which can be an individual or an organisation or the local youth office; and
- make adoption orders and other orders relating to the status of children.

Guardians are appointed where parental responsibility is removed or when a mother is single and under 18. Children over 14 can apply to the court to have their guardian changed as can parents, if they do not agree with the guardian appointed for their children.

The youth office is mandated to assist the courts in all matters pertaining to a child's safety and welfare and will be expected to aid with the investigation and to provide reports. Since individual social workers vary in their views on how this mandate is to be fulfilled there is an on-going debate between the courts, the youth office and the administration.

The question of legal representation of children and the rights of children born out of wedlock compared with those who are 'legitimate', will be addressed in future legislation as there is a general recognition that this needs urgent attention. (Report to UN Committee on Rights of the Child 1994 quoted in Ruxton, 1996).

## The interface with the legal system

There are no formal reporting systems for child abuse or neglect, no registers are kept and considerable discretion can be exercised before a case is taken to court. It is expected that children, particularly older children, are closely involved in decisions concerning their lives, counselling is directed at helping them to relinquish inappropriate responsibility. Their interest can be represented by adults of their choice, a guardian, friend or social workers from the agencies involved with them. If children request to be accommodated against their parents' wishes or need to be removed to a place of safety, the guardianship court has to be involved and the matter needs to be investigated by the judge as soon as possible. Social workers and youth workers from voluntary agencies can act as representatives and present reports to the court but the social worker from the youth office who is responsible for the patch in which a youngster or a family live, will be primarily responsible for court liaison and for reports to the judge. Representation of children in contested care cases is increasingly being requested as is the appointment of guardians ad litem in recognition of potential conflicts of interest between parents and children and welfare services and children.

# ITALY

## Getting help

The first port of call for a family seeking help might well be the locally based generic multi-disciplinary health and social service teams (*Unità Sanitaria Locale* — USL). Article 1 of law 184/83 states that, "A child has the right to be brought up within its own family", and the USLs are available to offer assistance to families in the rearing of their children. Families are free to accept or refuse this help.

Schools and nurseries frequently have psychologists, social pedagogues and medical services attached to them which are accessible to both children and their parents. There is also the possibility of help from hospital-based paediatric and social work services and 'neuro-psychiatric services for children' which are somewhat akin to child guidance clinics.

Italy has a range of voluntary welfare agencies and there is also a national child helpline (*Telefono Azzuro*) which has received many thousands of calls since its inception in 1987. (Minozzi & Tomassi, 1994).

Parents and relatives of a child can also have direct access to the procurator for juveniles or the youth court (see below).

## The administrative system

Local government in Italy has recently been decentralised from the state to the provinces/metropolitan areas and from these to the municipalities and communes, with the result that services are developing differently in different regions. Regional variations are also the product of differences between the relatively prosperous north of Italy and the less favoured south.

Social services are located along with health services in local multi-disciplinary teams (*Unità Sanitaria Locale* — USL). These have traditionally developed an "interdisciplinary, co-operative professional culture" (Saraceno & Negri, 1994). The social workers (*assistente sociale*) work generically and can refer families needing more specialist help to other agencies. There are a wide range of neuro-psychiatric and paediatric services. Some agencies also employ 'educators', specialists in work relating to the general development of children as opposed to their psychological problems. Psychologists are widely employed in the USLs, in the child guidance service and attached to schools. The school health service and its paediatricians seem to play a very active role.

There are two types of voluntary organisations, quite clearly distinguished by different regulations with regard to taxing and funding. One is the self-help organisations, the other those organisations which employ professional workers. Both are important in the system. There is currently an increase in contracting out, both to the 'not-for-profit' voluntary associations and the private sector. Many of the support services for work with children are voluntary organisations and many residential resources are run by the Church.

When a family is in temporary difficulty, social workers can, with the agreement of parents, place children in foster care for a period up to six months. For longer periods the court would need to be involved.

## The grounds for intervention

Social workers carry no particular responsibility for investigation in child abuse cases, and cannot themselves instigate formal legal proceedings. If, however, they are concerned about the safety of a child they, like other professionals, can submit a written report about their concerns to the procurator for juveniles (see below).

This report does not necessarily have to cite legally admissible evidence.

## The legal system

Child welfare is the province of the youth court (*Tribunale per i Minorenni* — TM). There is a tribunal for each region comprising a president, two salaried magistrates and two honorary magistrates. The honorary magistrates must have some special experience or expertise with children. They could thus be psychologists, psychiatrists, social workers or teachers.

The youth court has jurisdiction over three areas: civil, administrative and penal. Its proceedings are inquisitorial rather than adversarial.

Complementary to each tribunal is a procurator of the republic for minors (*procuratore della repubblica per i minorenni*). This office is responsible for promoting the judicial recognition and the practical implementation of the rights of minors. It is the procurator's office to which initial reports or referrals concerning children at risk would be made. The procurator can also be approached directly by family members or relatives. Upon receipt of a referral, the procurator can:

* separate children from their families in an emergency;
* refer the matter to the youth court;
* request further investigation, possibly by a social worker;
* consult with families informally, offering advice or suggestions. (These suggestions might carry considerable 'moral', although not 'legal' authority)

In each prefecture there is also a 'tutelary judge' (*giudice tutelare*). This office has the role of supervising guardianship and custody of minors and monitoring post-judicial decisions in relation to them. Where a child is without parents or a guardian, or if a court has removed parental powers, the tutelary judge appoints a guardian to be responsible for the child's care. This may be a relative or the local USL. The tutelary judge can also intervene in families to implement decisions of the youth court, and can involve other bodies (including social workers) in this.

## The interface with the legal system

The points within the system where legal and welfare issues most clearly intersect are located in the offices of the procurator and the tutelary judge. Respectively, they exercise both authority and discretion over the instigation and implementation of judicial proceedings: their interventions can thus fall into either or both the legal and administrative sphere. They are accessible to, and can consult informally with social workers, children and parents and in this way seek to mediate negotiated solutions to family problems.

# THE NETHERLANDS

## Getting help

Families in need of help are most likely to approach a non-governmental organisation in the first place. These provide most of the services for children and families, and according to the principles of subsidiarity they are supported and funded by local government. They provide both generic social services and specialist services for children and families. The network of services is complex and there are co-ordinating bodies at central and regional government level.

If an agency considers that a family needs more help than they are able to give themselves, they would be likely to look elsewhere in the NGO system for alternatives. Examples would be the youth advisory centres (JACs), the organisations for after school care and the guardianship organisations (see below). Another possibility would be the Regional Institutes for Ambulatory Mental Health (RIAGG), which provide outpatient psychiatric services.

## The administrative system

Most of the services for children and families are provided by the NGOs. They provide fieldwork, daycare, fostering and residential services for both the voluntary and legal systems. For example, the JACs provide a confidential counselling service for children and young people aged 12 to 25. There are after school care organisations which include the parents in their programme. The guardianship organisations provide a social work service for the courts and also work with families on a voluntary basis. The larger non-governmental organisations may run a range of different services, some voluntary, some statutory.

The confidential doctor service (CDS) was set up as a non-governmental organisation. It now has an official connection to the child care and protection board (see below), and has official responsibilities for collecting statistics in relation to child protection. It continues to fulfil its original function of providing a confidential co-ordinating system of services for families in difficulties, with the aim of avoiding referral into the legal system. The service is confidential both to the person making a referral and the referred. Anyone can tell the confidential doctor service about a family where they think that a child may be being abused. The service will then make investigations, without in the first place informing the parents, into the circumstances and reality of the allegation. When the family is approached, work is on a voluntary basis. The confidential doctor service is usually a co-ordinator rather than a provider of services.

The Ministry of Justice administers the judicial child protection system and the child care and protection board. There are local offices of the board to which referrals can be made by officials, parents and members of the public. The social workers of the child care and protection board make inquiries into allegations of abuse, and can refer cases to the judge for children. Members of the family can also apply to the judge for a family supervision order.

## Grounds for intervention

The non-governmental organisations provide services according to the aims and objectives of their parent organisation. Municipal authorities are responsible for a range of facilities for young people and for child care policy. They have to ensure that there is a provision of generic social services in their area.

Legal intervention is based on the need to protect children and help parents to care for them where the care given by the parents puts the child's development at risk. (*Ministerie van Justitie*, 1992). The child care and protection board can ask for a child protection order if it believes that the welfare of the child is under threat and that this is the only way in which help can be given. (*Ministrie van Justitie*, 1993).

## The legal system

The legal system for children is inquisitorial, welfare based and includes juvenile justice for children up to 12 years. Children's judges have the same training as other judges. The court hearing is informal, and the parents and child are able to talk directly to the judge. There is provision for legal aid and legal representation.

A written report has to be made by the child care and protection board which is discussed with the parents (and the child if 16 or over). The parents (and child) can make comments which will be submitted with the report.

There are four orders that the judge can make:

- a family supervision order;
- an order suspending parental rights;
- an order terminating parental rights (which may be referred to as a 'care order'); and
- an emergency protection order.

The family supervision order is more extensive than supervision orders (or similar) in other countries. It gives responsibility for a child to a guardian (also sometimes called a family supervisor), who can decide where the child should live, and whose advice the parents have to take notice of. A family supervision order lasts for a year and can be renewed for a year at a time. Under the orders suspending or terminating parental rights, a child will be placed in the care of a guardianship board. Under an emergency protection order, a child will be placed in the care of the child care and protection board.

Emergency orders can be made by the judge for children on the application of the child care and protection board.

## The interface with the legal system

The child care and protection board and the confidential doctor service are the intermediaries between the administrtative and the legal systems. Recent legislation has introduced more formality into the system in various ways, and the confidential doctor service has recently become administratively connected to the organisation of the child care and protection board. The confidential doctor service has a role in deflecting families from legal intervention by encouragement and persuasion to voluntary engagement, but does not have the mediation and negotiating position of the Flemish mediation committee or the Francophone *conseiller*. The child care and protection board provides an investigative body which does not necessarily refer cases into the legal arena, but is nevertheless the main route into the legal system. It does not have an explicit role in avoiding or preventing referral.

## THE UK — ENGLAND

## Getting help

The social services department area children and families team would be the most likely place for a family to seek help or be referred for help. There are voluntary agencies who also offer help to families with problems, but not many. An alternative possibility would be referral via their general practitioner to a child and family guidance clinic. In the social services department it would be most likely that the family would be seen initially by a duty social worker. They would not be allocated a social worker immediately. The help on offer would be practical help, limited short-term financial help in an emergency, advice and short-term counselling. Extensive support from family workers and other social work involvement would be possible in serious situations. Referral from the social services department to a voluntary organisation would be a possibility in some areas.

## The administrative system

Local government is the main provider of services for children and families through children and family area teams of the social services department. Local authority social workers work closely with the police in child protection investigations (see below), and there are joint police/social services child protection teams. There is also a school social work service run by the local authority education department, concerned mainly with school attendance and student welfare. Health visitors are part of the community health system which is not run by the local authority. Within the social service department, work with children and families where there are general concerns or child protection issues is usually undertaken by the children and family team. Work with children and families where there are issues of delinquent and anti-social behaviour, and where the courts are involved, is undertaken by the juvenile justice team. The local authority usually also runs a generic 'out-of-hours' duty team.

There are a range of voluntary agencies, national and local. These mainly offer services under contract to the local authority, but some are also open to referral from elsewhere, or direct approach by the family. Voluntary agencies run residential homes and fostering schemes, family centres, assessment centres and offer counselling and support. There are a few agencies based in the community set up by parents for parents.

The social services department is also able to buy in the services of privately run (profit-making) services, such as residential child care and counselling for children.

Central government does not run any services for children and families, but has set up a system for the co-ordination of the services involved with children in relation to child protection. In each area there has to be an area child protection committee (ACPC). The local authority social services department, the

police, the community health services and the education services
are represented on the committee. The ACPC is responsible for
the overall effectiveness of the co-ordination of child protection in
their area. Co-ordination takes place through child protection
conferences, which are case conferences attended by the professionals involved in the case in question, their line managers, the
parents (unless there are exceptional reasons against this), and if
appropriate, the child. The child protection conference is usually
initiated and organised by the social services department. Its task
is to share information and decide whether a child should be put
on the child protection register of 'children at risk' in various
categories of abuse. If the child is registered, the conference has to
appoint a key worker and decide on a plan for the child's
protection. The conference cannot make decisions about resources
or about taking legal proceedings, but its discussions are inevitably
extremely influential in these respects. After the initial conference, further conferences take place at regular intervals, usually
six monthly, until the conference is able to decide that the child's
name can be removed from the register.

## The grounds for intervention

The social services department is legitimated to provide services
for children and families where the child is defined under the
Children Act 1989 as being 'in need'. The definition of 'in need' is
in terms of being able to achieve 'a reasonable standard of health
or development'. (Children Act 1989 s.17 (10)). The interpretation varies between different authorities.

The local authority also has a duty to investigate where they
'have reasonable cause to expect that a child... is suffering or is
likely to suffer significant harm'. (Children Act 1989 s.47 (1)).

The grounds for referral to the judicial system are that a child 'is
suffering or is likely to suffer from significant harm', which can be
attributed to the care given not being that expected of a reasonable
parent. (Children Act 1989 s.31 (2)).

## The legal system

The legal system is adversarial; the judge is arbitrator between the
two parties, the local authority, which is the only body able to
apply for an order, and the parents. The welfare of the child is the
paramount concern of the court, but the rights of both parents and
children are also important. The court system is entirely separate
from the system for juvenile justice.

The court hearings are formal, and conducted by lawyers.

Parents can give evidence, and can ask to be heard, but they are usually represented by their lawyers. Children similarly can be heard, but they are represented by their guardian ad litem and lawyers. Social workers have to give evidence and have the opportunity to explain their views, but their case is presented and shaped by the lawyers of the local authority.

Magistrates in the family proceedings courts are lay workers; they have specific training for work in these courts. Judges in the higher level of the family proceedings courts have the same background as other judges and are appointed by the same system.

The orders that can be made are:

- placement away from the parents (care orders and residence orders);
- supervision orders (where the child remains at home);
- secure accommodation orders (where the child is placed for a limited period in a restricted environment);
- child assessment orders (to compel the parents to bring the child for a medical, psychiatric or social assessment);
- emergency protections orders; and
- contact orders (regulating the level of contact that parents should be allowed with children on placement).

Supervision orders cannot be for longer than one year, but can be reviewed. Care orders are not time limited. Cases do not return for further review, and may not be seen by the same judge or magistrates at each hearing.

## The interface with the legal system

The system of the child protection conference and registration is within the administrative system because it is voluntary. It has no power to compel parents to agree with recommendations and it does not have the power to refer into the judicial system. It exists parallel to the judicial system rather than connecting with it. In many respects it shows the influence of the judicial system in the formality of its proceedings and its concern with establishing facts; it is frequently attended by the legal department of the local authority who would be involved in any subsequent decision to take legal proceedings.

Referral to the judicial system can take place independently of the conference system. If a child is on a judicial placement order, s/he will no longer be registered, and the child protection conference will not be involved any further, unless there are renewed problems following a return home. The move into the judicial system is a highly charged event, which brings the family into contact with a new set of professionals. They will be involved with the solicitor who represents the parents (unless they decide against representation), the solicitor who represents their child and the guardian ad litem, an independent social worker appointed by the court to represent the child's best interests and convey to the court the child's wishes and feelings. In most situations, there will be a period of at least three months uncertainty between the initial and the final court hearings.

## THE UK — SCOTLAND

### Getting help

The family would be most likely to go to the generic services of the local authority social services department. There are some voluntary agencies that might be approached, and the Royal Scottish Society for the Prevention of Cruelty to Children would be one of these. The Childwatch telephone service would also be available. It would also be possible for a family to go in the first place to the reporter, though this would be less likely. The social services department would be able to offer advice, practical help and specialist family workers. They could also make referrals to child guidance or to voluntary agencies.

### The administrative system

The social work services provided by local government are the main framework of the system of help and support for families on a voluntary basis. They run, or are responsible for the inspection of, residential and fostering services and they provide field work and day care services. There is a system of inter-professional case discussions and child protection registers. At the point when there are serious anxieties about a child, the social workers would call a multi-disciplinary case conference, which might be attended by parents. The conference has to decide whether the child's name should be put on the child protection register and whether the case should be referred to the reporter; it has to identify a key worker and the aims of work with the family and discuss the prosecution of the offender.

Voluntary agencies also contribute to services for children, and the RSSPCC has a statutory role, though this is limited, and its social workers do not have the same powers and responsibilities as local authority social workers.

## The grounds for intervention

The ground for administrative intervention have recently been changed. Since the Children (Scotland) Act 1995, the local authority has a duty to safeguard and promote the welfare of 'children in need'. Under previous legislation, the duty was a wider one — to promote the welfare of all people in their area.

The grounds for compulsory intervention are that the child is suffering or at risk of suffering from significant harm and that the parents have a responsibility for this which they are not meeting.

## The legal system

The legal system is inquisitorial, and children's hearings concentrate exclusively on matters of child welfare once questions of fact and justice have been settled. The sheriff works primarily in the adult criminal justice system, and is an experienced and qualified lawyer. The sheriff hears evidence from the reporter and parents in closed court, and makes a decision as to whether the grounds have been proved in order for a hearing to proceed. If there is an appeal, the sheriff has the right to substitute his own decision for any decision that the children's hearing might have made.

If the sheriff establishes the grounds for intervention, the reporter calls another children's hearing for the panel to make a disposal. In all cases, because there may be an actual or potential conflict of interest between the child and the parents, the panel must consider appointing a safeguarder to protect the child's best interests.

The panel may make a range of supervision orders, some requiring foster or residential care, and residential assessment orders for up to 21 days.

In an emergency, a child protection order can be granted by the sheriff.

## The interface with the legal system

At the point where judicial referral might be necessary, the children's hearing system becomes involved. The children's hearings are co-ordinated by reporters, employed by the children's reporter administration. Reporters normally have previous experience as either lawyers or social workers. Referrals are made to the reporter by professionals, private individuals and by children themselves. On receipt of the referral, the reporter must decide whether the grounds of the referral can be established and if the child is in need of compulsory measures of care. He can then either take no action, refer the family back to the social work department, or bring the child before a children's hearing. The children's panel is made up of three panel members, drawn from members of the public selected and trained by a local authority advisory committee. The hearing is attended by the child and parents, the reporter and the social worker. If the grounds for the referral are denied, the case passes to the sheriff. If the sheriff establishes the grounds, the case comes back to the children's hearing for an order to be made. If he does not, there is no further intervention.

# Chapter 5:
# Eight European child protection systems — themes and comparisons

In this chapter we consider:

- some of the main findings of the study about similarities and differences between the eight systems;
- the overall responses of English workers to the other systems, and the overall responses of the continental and Scottish practitioners to the English system; and
- in the boxes, some key underlying concepts which help to understand the character of continental systems.

No two systems or their associated practices are exactly alike, and any attempt at a classifactory schema is in danger of obscuring as much as it reveals. In Chapter 6 we discuss the analysis of similarities and differences between systems in detail. Nevertheless, it is possible to isolate structural and cultural features which are common to all systems, and a number of axes for comparison and analysis which help to reveal certain family resemblances. The theoretical position developed in previous work which compared French and English child protection work (Cooper *et al.*, 1995) tends to be confirmed — that in any particular system the inter-relationship of social structure, history, professional and political culture and the division of professional labour interlock to create a unique phenomena — is carried forward in the present book. Comparison works best as a method for revealing the internal characteristics of systems and in particular how, on closer examination, apparently identical practices or principles in different systems are divergent, because each is inflected by its relationship to connected features within the system. In this chapter, however, we are painting a broad picture. The more subtle and differentiated features of different systems emerge in the succeeding chapters.

---

**Box 1**
*Subsidiarity*
*Subsidiarity* is an important principle of political life in many northern European countries, particularly Germany, the Netherlands and Belgium. The principle is strongly influenced by Catholic social teaching which in turn has played a powerful shaping role in social life in many continental states. Subsidiarity means that whatever smaller and more localised institutions or groups can do on their own must not be removed by a higher level of competence or by the power of the state. Responsibility and decision-making should rest with the people most directly involved. At the same time the state should support local or regional institutions in develop-.ing strong social networks, and in fact this is an obligation on the German state.

---

We begin by outlining the range of features which do appear to be common to all the systems we studied. These commonalities emerge at a relatively high-level of abstraction and are no doubt to be explained by reference to shared historical, religious, spatial and socio-economic factors which have characterised the development of welfare within liberal-capitalist European nation states since the second world war.

## Shared features of the eight systems

We found that there were some common factors amongst the diversity of systems and agencies which we met with. Some of these can be considered as structural similarities and some as cultural.

## Structural similarities

- A judicial system run by the state which includes the part of the judicial system relation to children.
- A division of the provision of social work services between voluntary and statutory agencies.
- Universal education from the age of five/six, but nursery school provision varied.

- A health system available to all, either through insurance or free at point of use; but a universal health visiting service does not exist everywhere.
- A local government system that provides some part of the administrative system of child welfare and child protection.
- A network of voluntary organisations that provide some part of the administrative system for child welfare and child protection.

---

**Box 2**
**Welfare pluralism**
Subsidiarity is not the state 'washing its hands' of responsibility for the civil or family domain, but rather encouraging *pluralism* in the realm of welfare, and autonomy for social institutions concerned with social life. This helps explain both the greater involvement of 'independent sector' organisations in child care and protection in these countries, and their strength and ubiquity. In Germany, Flanders and France for example, public and 'private' agencies are strongly interwoven, and there is much less central government control or management of social work practice. In turn this may help explain the greater degree of individual professional autonomy which continental social workers are often perceived by British practitioners to take for granted. Subsidiarity is partly conceived as a buttress against the threat of a 'corporatist' state, and it is arguable that the degree of central government control of child protection work in Britain is a manifestation of such corporatism.

---

In all countries we were looking at the effect of the different ways of managing the division of child protection between the law and administration, and between the statutory and the voluntary agencies. We were looking at the effect on child protection of some differences in universal provision in the context that there was a high degree of similarity between the social structures of the countries concerned. In the following accounts of the research findings in the different countries, these similarities need to be borne in mind.

## Cultural comparisons

There were also important similarities in the professional culture of social workers in all these countries. The code of ethics which the social workers' responses embodied seemed to be the same. All the social workers seemed to work on the basis that:

- social work intervention should aim to promote independence: 'doing with, not doing to';

- confidentiality should be maintained. The details of when and why there might be exceptions to this varied. This similarity therefore masked important differences;

- making and maintaining a relationship with clients was an important aspect of their work;

- social work practice is based on knowledge from social sciences;

- the situations of their clients were complex and not easily understood;

- there was a potential for child abuse in many families; and that

- there was a relationship between child behaviour and family behaviour.

There were also shared assumptions that went beyond professional culture and suggested a shared European expectation that:

- children have rights;

- children should be brought up by their parents;

- families should be kept together;

- there is a point at which intervention to separate children from their families is justified and that

- the state or community should be able to intervene to this effect.

However, the point at which any one of these expectations should override another varied. There are many interpretations of the statement that children have rights, and many aspects of the statement to interpret. In different countries the global statement which all would support, has different meanings and takes its place within different priorities. The point at which it is decided that a family should no longer be kept together depends on the concept of the family that is being used. In all countries, the state could intervene, but the grounds for state intervention vary both qualitatively and quantitatively. It is important to be aware of the similarities, but closer examination of similarities usually leads to a new awareness of difference.

---

**Box 3**
*Solidarity and the family*
Subsidiarity is hard to make sense of in British terms without the associated idea of **solidarity**. Mutuality, reciprocity of obligations and duties, social responsibility, social cohesion are all elements of the idea of solidarity. The strength of local social institutions, non-governmental organisations (NGOs) and welfare networks would be a part measure of solidarity and social cohesion. Subsidiarity means that solidarity is hierarchically ordered, with the main source of solidarity resting in the family, secondly in the community, and lastly in the state. The picture which emerges is of progressively widening circles of responsibility, and diminishing influence on personal life with social distance. This means that the *family* may be conceived in a fundamentally different way in continental societies shaped by these principles. It is not primarily or only a private domain which should be free of interference unless some transgression is identified. Rather it is a foundation of society and social solidarity and a proper object of social concern, support, and welfare. The interests of the state and of the family in general coincide. Of the countries with which we are concerned this emerges most clearly in France, where the family may be thought of as a kind of model for political life, and as an essential building block of a strong republic.

---

However, the ways in which the different systems were structured and the ways in which they actually operated, suggested that different cultures interpret these assumptions very differently, and deal with the conflicts between them very differently.

## Common features of systems — discussion

### The judiciary

All the child protection systems are embedded within a judicial system administered by the state at national level. However, in those countries with a federal system of government (e.g. Belgium or Germany), there may be some variations in the judicial system at regional or communal level. Scotland and England, while both are politically part of the United Kingdom, have different legal systems which lead to different practices, procedures and decision-making processes in the judicial sphere of child protection.

## The Statutory and voluntary sectors

In all systems there is a division in the provision of services between voluntary or independent agencies and statutory bodies. Statutory bodies are frequently organised at local or regional levels of government, as with English and Scottish local authorities or French *conseils generaux*, with powers devolved from central government to locally elected bodies. The role of voluntary organisations and the scope of their operations varies widely and is significantly a function of national historical factors. The subsidiarity principle in Germany, the Netherlands and Belgium has secured a leading role for the independent sector in these countries. The powerful *secteur associatif* is equally significant in considering French child protection work even though subsidiarity is not a fundamental aspect of the French system. Many French *associations* undertake statutory work on behalf of the courts on a contractual basis. Although it would be unwise to use the statutory/voluntary division of labour in the United Kingdom as a model for understanding other European countries, in all cases there is a division of labour along this axis, which it is important to grasp in considering any particular country's child protection system.

## Education and pre-school education

All countries in the study provide universal education from the age of five or six and professional relationships with teachers and other educational staff may become significant in child protection work. Levels of pre-school provision vary considerably and this has wide-ranging consequences for child protection and family support in different countries. France has universal state pre-school provision for three to six year olds while in England approximately 35 per cent of children in the same age band have access to publically funded nursery provision. The likelihood of child abuse in young children coming to early professional attention is obviously significantly improved the greater the professional contact. Effective 'surveillance' and 'detection' (very British concepts) are one variable, levels of 'family support' another.

---

**Box 4**
**Republicanism**
**Republicanism** is a strong organising principle in many
European countries, even though some, like Belgium, also
have a monarchy. The powerful element of paternalism in
French social life, reflected in the wide ranging powers of the
children's judge and the ease with which the law may be
invoked in child protection matters, is balanced by definite
obligations and commitments on the part of the state to
enhance and support families. When children and parents
meet with a judge in a French *audience* there is a sense that
everybody has some ownership of the 'space', even if not
everyone possesses equal powers in the situation. The family
has obligations, but so does the state who is embodied by the
judge. Negotiated reciprocity within the framework of the
law is the organising principle of such meetings. Thus ideas
about the private and public, intervention and
non-intervention, are framed differently for families and
practitioners in countries with a republican tradition.

---

### Health provision

Universal health services were a feature of all the countries we
researched, although modes of organisation, delivery and funding
vary greatly, and levels of community health provision also
differed. The role of the medical profession in child protection
work shows significant variations however. In the great majority of
countries, community nursing services may play an important part
in family support and detection of abuse. In Belgium and the
Netherlands the confidential doctor services (and *SOS Enfance*)
are usually outside mainstream health services, but with medical
input or leadership. The history and character of this service is
different in the two countries, and does not signal the 'medicalis-
ation' of child abuse on a treatment model which has sometimes
been feared, encouraged, or mythologised in the Anglo-American
context.

### Professional culture

Professional culture is a complex and ambiguous concept. It can be
simultaneously understood as an independent variable which
interacts with others to contribute to the total character of a
system, or as a dependent variable which needs to be largely
explained by reference to other system characteristics. The

methodology of this study involves studying instances of professional culture — the behaviour, thought, belief systems, interactional patterns of a professional group — and trying to understand, interpret and explain this by reference to other known features of child protection systems. Although we were able to isolate distinctive cultural characteristics in each of the national groups we researched, certain common assumptions and approaches were evident.

Different European intellectual and pedagogical traditions inform the training and education of social workers in different parts of the continent. *Éducation* (France) and social pedagogy (Germany, Flanders, Holland, Italy, Belgium) appear highly distinctive to a practitioner trained in the rather more diffuse educational culture of an English or Scottish university social work department. In recent years the professional culture of English, and to a slightly lesser extent, Scottish social work has been the object of concerted pressure for change. Some of this pressure, for example the introduction of competency based training models and ministerial attack on anti-discriminatory practice, has been clearly intended while some has been the unintended consequence of professional and wider social reaction to public anxiety about child abuse and protection in these countries.

The impact of these cultural changes on the English professionals in our study appeared marked, and when mirrored back through the clear differences of culture among their foreign counterparts, became a subject of reflection and commentary for them. Thus while English practitioners shared in the common values and practice principles outlined below, they were more often in tension and competition with other imperatives deriving from this 'imposed culture', than they were for the continental and Scottish workers. A farrago of legalism, proceduralism, managerialism, and more than a whiff of commercialism are the major elements which combine to tend to deflect English social workers from sustaining a clear focus on the needs of the child and the wider family in favour of procedural or legal rectitude and resource led managerial hard headedness. In our report of the initial phase of Anglo-French comparative research (Cooper *et al.*, 1992), we noted how

...the balance between 'social work discourse' and 'legal discourse' in the English group discussions reveals that the latter frequently supplants the former, and is introduced to curtail its development... It is as if, in the course of group discussions, voices, pleading for ('traditional' social work values) are dismissed by others asserting the primacy of legal imperatives. (p.22).

In the present study we are able to point to numerous parallel processes in English groups, except that procedural discourse has to a significant extent replaced, or entered the arena alongside, legal discourse. In one group heated discussion between practitioners from different local authority departments about what would or should 'trigger' a Section 47 Children Act investigation dominated for considerable periods. In another, the local authority's 'eligibility criteria' for receiving a service were a strong focal point of discussion, led by the team manager. These preoccupations reflect contemporary English realities, and illustrate how certain characteristics of post-Children Act professional culture tend to subordinate the professional will to 'think about the case' first and consider organisational limits to offering help and protection afterwards.

With this caveat, practitioners in all the countries studied seemed to share in the following assumptions and principles.

- Social work intervention should aim to promote the independence and autonomy of families and individuals. Practitioners were concerned to work 'with' or 'alongside' children and parents and not 'do to' them. Making and sustaining trusting relationships with clients was seen as a primary medium of successful intervention, and where there was a possibility that coercive intervention might compromise trust, practitioners everywhere were concerned to think carefully about how to minimise its impact. Thus although practitioners in all countries worked with awareness of a potential need for coercion, facilitative and enabling relationships in which professional or moral (rather than legal) authority might still play a part, were seen as the *sine qua non* of the social work role.
- Preserving confidentiality of client material was understood to be of central importance by practitioners in all countries. However, limits to confidentiality were equally clearly identified in all countries, although some particular services, such as confidential doctor centres, appear to operate with a near absolute commitment to the principle. Limits to confidentiality of individual client information appear to be set by judicial parameters — the need to produce evidence, information or grounds in a court hearing under either civil or criminal law — and for some systems by procedure, in cases where formal sharing of information is required by administrative procedures, such as English and Scottish case conferences. In more

rights-based systems, confidentiality is explicitly seen as a right, but quickly comes into tension with the rights of other parties to the situation. In more apparently child-centred systems, or services within welfare orientated systems, (such as confidential doctor services) the right to confidentiality for children is implicit but overall subordinate to wider considerations of child welfare, such as maximising reporting and co-operation. In more family oriented systems like France, child or adult confidentiality may again be subordinate to wider professional aims like working for change in families so that children will be better protected within them.

- Social work practice is based on knowledge from the social sciences in all countries. We did not research the training and education of practitioners in detail in this study, but an identifiable core of social and psychological concepts were deployed by social workers in all countries to understand and think about the case. These were derived from: family systems theory, child development theory, counselling theory, and rather more implicitly, psychoanalysis and general systems theory; feminist perspectives within these approaches were influential. Practitioners in all countries thought in terms of a relationship between child behaviour and parental/family behaviour, and this understanding was usually expressed in identifiable systemic language.

---

**Box 5**
*Intermediate institutions*
Taken together these principles help to account for the existence of strong *intermediate institutions* in these societies. In the child protection field, the Flemish mediation committee is a good example. The committee was conceived simultaneously as an alternative to judicial intervention in child care and juvenile crime, as a buffer between the administrative and legal domains, and as a filter through which cases must pass if they are to reach the courts. The committee is a politically sanctioned body, which partly acts to preserve the realm of civil life from undue or unnecessary intrusion by the state or the courts, while discharging clear responsibilities in matters of social and public concern. In this sense the committee is an embodiment of the subsidiarity principle.

---

In the light of comments above about divergence in national professional cultures, we would observe that these concepts and theories are differentially inflected by broader pedagogic principles and national cultural trends. Thus, for example, attachment theory and the work of Bowlby informs social work thinking about child development and needs in England, France and Scotland, but policies and practices with respect to enforced separation differ markedly. *Education* and the valorisation of the biological family in France reinforces family policy which keeps children in families of origin, while ideas about psychological parenting and permanency lead to more children being placed outside families in England. Both would deploy attachment theory to justify and conceptualise practice decisions.

• Practitioners in all countries saw the family situation in the case study as complex and not easily understood. The group discussion phase of the methodology frequently encompassed much broader reflection on the general complexity of family predicaments, the social work task, and current debates within the profession. There appeared to be a widespread assumption that child abuse could occur in any type of family, although the scope of administrative and judicial definitions of abuse varies among countries.

Practitioners sometimes made explicit reference to research evidence about child abuse and protection, but their mode of responding to the case, as distinct from the knowledge base which they brought to bear upon it, was remarkably consistent and there was a sense of familiarity for groups when watching their foreign counterparts engaged in discussion. Local variations and anomolies in research group composition make it difficult to generalise, but discussions in all countries tended to have an open-ended and open-minded quality in which there was an implicit assumption that understanding and decision-making is best achieved through dialogic and deliberative approaches, rather than appeal to received authority, uni-dimensional explanatory models, or imperatives of political correctness.

## The practitioners' views of each other's systems and practices — a summary

In the following section we summarise common features of responses of the various English groups to the range of other systems and the common features of the responses of practitioners in all other systems to the English system and practices.

### English practitioners' views of the other systems

After hearing about the system of the other country and seeing their video, the social workers discussed their views on this different way of doing things. They began by seeing the similarities that there were in the way that they and their foreign colleagues approached the case. They noted the similar concerns about the possibility of sexual abuse and the possible connection between marital violence and Andrew's violent behaviour. They saw themselves as using the same theories in relation to family functioning. As they considered the action that the foreign social workers thought of taking, they began to uncover the differences. These related to the differences in the social work role and the different action that the different legal and administrative structures enabled the social workers to take. They noted the freedom of social workers in other countries from the duty to investigate, and related this to their own difficulty in setting up a working relationship with parents. This led to reflections on their own system and the effect on their work of the pressure of media criticism and of administrative requirements to follow procedures.

The English groups tended to see other systems as:

- more flexible;
- offering more support to social workers in taking risks;
- putting more pressure on parents;
- being less aware of parental rights to information and consultation;
- relying less on evidence;
- being less bureaucratic; and
- having a more 'user friendly' legal system (for both families and social workers).

---

**Box 6**
**Rights and social rights**
The concept of **rights** in matters involving the family and the state is different in many continental countries when compared with the Anglo-American tradition. The last fifteen years have witnessed a consolidation of ideologies of individual rights in Britain, and a general decline in ideas of collective responsibility. However the differences betweeen Britain and other European countries have much deeper historical roots than this, and are not simply a by-product of Thatcherism-cum-Majorism. Republicanism, solidarity, and subsidiarity are grounded in a set of assumptions about the relationship of the individual to society and government

which yield social practices embodying *social rights*. Thus the individual's 'right' to family support does not have to be 'claimed' in quite the same way which it may be in England — it is just assumed by all involved. Equally, if the family rather than the individual is taken to be a basic unit, and hence a bearer of rights, then conflicts of rights between family members are likely to be subordinated to questions of 'family welfare'. To English eyes it may seem that children's (or parents') rights are neglected because of this, but from a continental perspective it may equally appear that the primacy of family relationships, or social cohesion, are neglected within our paradigm.

English practitioners noticed that the foreign groups spent *more time discussing how they would work with the family* and very little time discussing procedural or legal aspects of the case.

The English social workers saw their own system as *heavily proceduralised*. They shared a commitment to children and therefore wanted to accept the emphasis on child protection. They also felt strongly about individual rights. The problem for them was that the rights of the parents were in conflict with the needs of the children. The rhetoric of the procedures enjoined them both to protect children and to respect parental rights. The only way that they could deal with this was by following procedures rigorously — but this then went against their professional opinion as to how they should be working. There was a general concern about the amount of emphasis placed on following the right procedures, and the effect that this had on their ability to establish relationships with the families they worked with. There was considerable criticism of the effect that an anxiety about following correct procedures could have on their practice.

The English social workers saw the systems of the other countries as concentrating on the family *at the risk of failing to protect the child*, and at the same time, as too ready to override the rights of parents. The family was seen as taking precedence over individuals, whether child or parent. At the same time, the English social workers seemed to envy their colleagues the working situation that their systems created for them, and to see less conflict for them in achieving their goals. They certainly envied their colleagues the lack of media attention and criticism. It seemed to them as though social workers working in other systems were less open to criticism and better supported within their agencies. The English social workers felt that they had to make sure that they followed procedures correctly to protect themselves.

---

**Box 7**

**Rights and family support**

From recent research which compared the experiences of French and English families who had been the subjects of child protection interventions (Baistow *et al.*, 1996), it emerged that French parents who expected to receive help, were often successful in arguing for different forms of help than that which was offered, but were much less clear about how the system worked and where professionals fitted in to it. English parents more often felt they had to fight to get help, were frightened of the power of professionals, but were well-informed about the functioning of the system. On the whole they wanted more intervention, not less. Being well-informed seemed to reflect English social workers' concern to tell families their rights, and to transmit information as an aspect of promoting clients' rights. However, English (and French) parents did not emerge as especially concerned about their 'rights', but as preoccupied with securing their own and their children's welfare.

---

Although many of the English participants felt that the *rights of the parents* were not sufficiently safeguarded in the other European systems, there was also support for the view that concern for the rights of parents sometimes prevented social workers in this country from protecting children, and that the emphasis placed on rights sometimes prevented social workers from helping families. It was as if, in the concern over individual rights and protective procedures, something real to the families got lost.

In all English groups there seemed to be an element of *pride in the standards* that were expected and in the drive to protect children and put their interests first. There were often criticisms of the practice and lack of interagency procedures of other countries. At the same time, there was in all groups considerable envy for the social workers in other countries. It seemed as though in other countries, their colleagues worked within a framework of law and procedure that gave them a great deal more freedom to work in partnership with families and achieve change.

---

**Box 8**
**The citizen and the state**
Differences in the basic conception of the relationship
between the *citizen and the state* are sometimes traced back
to the work of key political theorists in each country, Thomas
Hobbes in England and Jean Jacques Rousseau in France.
Hobbes believed that the state, or the sovereign, was an
essential authority to regulate the competitive and self-
seeking tendencies of individuals. Thus his idea of the 'social
contract' and of law was negative. It exists by consent to
prevent unlimited self-assertion of individuals against each
other, and civilisation is based on fear rather than natural
sociability. Before the state is brought into being, there are
no moral or social obligations on individuals. One can see in
this the roots of a concept of the state as external to the
private sphere of family life, stepping in only to regulate
transgressive behaviour. By contrast Rousseau thought that
the state should express the general will of the majority
population and should be called to account by the people
when it failed to realise this will. Direct democracy involves
no loss of freedom since the people elect the government,
and law is not an external command sanctioned by force, but
the expression of each individual's 'higher self'. The state
gives political expression to the social character of human
beings, and one can see here the roots of modern French
social work practices in which families assume that 'the
state', in the form of the children's judge for example, should
make help available, and in which the judge must by law
attempt to gain the parents' agreement to measures which
s/he enforces. 'Rights' take on an entirely different meaning
in the context of such assumptions about the inherently social
character of individual behaviour or predicaments.

---

There is a considerable contrast between the responses of the
English social workers to the case outline and those of other
countries. The English social workers seem more conflicted and
anxious about the material than their foreign colleagues. They
faced the following dilemmas which the social workers in other
countries did not share.

- They could not act without evidence, and without information from the family they could not get evidence.
- From their knowledge and understanding of families and of child behaviour, they had grounds for anxiety about the children which did not constitute evidence.
- They needed information from Frances to be able to protect her, but would then have to break confidentiality.
- They had no way of compelling the parents to allow them access to Andrew, but without access to him, they could not assess his needs.

In spite of the differences in their systems, the social workers from other European countries shared several possibilities that made it a great deal easier for them to act.

- They did not have a legal duty to investigate, and therefore approached the parents on a different basis.
- They did not have to find evidence of harm in order to act.
- Parental non-co-operation could be a reason for referral, rather than preventing it.
- They could talk to children without having to get parental consent if this was necessary for the welfare of the child (except in Italy).
- They could offer confidentiality to a child.

### Core responses of foreign practitioners to the English system

The following reactions to the English system and its practices were common to all foreign groups.

- Practitioners spent little time talking about the family and the children in their own right, and did not concentrate much attention on reaching an understanding of the family's problems.
- Practitioners did not use theory or concepts very freely or confidently as tools for understanding the family.
- The needs and suffering of the children received comparatively little attention or understanding in their own right.
- Procedural and evidential discussion aimed at locating available information within an agency framework of responsibility occupied much time, in place of thinking about how the family works, and how to work with the family.
- Practitioners appeared to become rapidly ensnared in managing the tension between their investigative duty and their treatment or therapeutic objectives.
- The system appeared to encourage, or fail to defuse, conflict

between professionals and families, and as a consequence
tended to accentuate the controlling or policing functions of
social workers where parents are unco-operative.

---

**Box 9**
**Ideologies of training**
These organising principles of social and political life are
reflected in some of the underlying *ideologies of social work
practice and training*. In France the concept of *éducation* and
in other countries of social pedagogy both embody a holistic
conception of the individual and his or her social being. A
French *éducatrice* conceives of her role in relation to a child's
total social, emotional, developmental and family situation,
and her direct practice reflects this. It is easy to idealise
principles like these from a British perspective, particularly
when the whole idea of 'the social' has sometimes been
thrown into question by government in recent years. Although they help to organise and sustain a political commitment to social bonds and cohesion, they constitute no
automatic safeguard against poverty, unemployment,
racism, inequality — or child abuse, and may even serve to
prevent a sharp focus on what is happening to children in
families. In some cases one can find parallel notions in
British life which may encourage forms of social or professional strength that are relatively weak in continental
countries. But it helps to bear in mind these principles when
trying to 'enter' the way of thinking of practitioners in these
countries.

---

### Core responses of English workers to the other systems

The English groups displayed a range of common anxieties about
the foreign systems:

- that parents' rights were not protected or attended to;
- that action could be taken without evidence of abuse or harm;
- that foreign practitioners spent much time discussing family
  functioning and dynamics, but much less time planning any
  clear course of action; and
- that practitioners took unacceptable risks with respect to the
  safety of children, from the perspective of English practice.

However, by the end of group discussions, English workers
tended to agree that the child protection social work role in foreign

systems appears to be *easier* than in England. Ease of access to the legal sphere, relative legal informality and flexibility, separation between investigation and intervention, and a relative absence of conflicts of individual rights in favour of prioritising children's needs, appeared to be the principal factors which combine to produce this overall response.

## Some main differences in the eight systems

The main differences between the systems are summarised in terms of the judicial sphere and the administrative spheres, and with respect to how social workers viewed the desirability and feasibility of using compulsory powers in the research case study. The analysis of responses in terms of the use of compulsion serves as one important index of some central anomolies of the English system by comparison with the other seven.

### The judicial sphere of the eight systems

As this grid below demonstrates, there are very significant differences between the English system and the six continental systems. The Scottish system lies somewhere in between.

All countries except England have *professionally trained judges* for all work with children. In some countries, but not all, they have specialist training. The Scottish children's panels have lay workers, but they do not have the same status in the legal system as the English magistrate.

All systems except the English have an *inquisitorial legal system*. The English system has changed with the implimentation of the Children Act 1989, but it remains adversarial in construction and requires an adversarial framework for presenting information.

## Figure 1: Key legal characteristics of child protection systems

| JUDICIAL | B(FL) | B(Fr) | Fr | G | I | N | S | E |
|---|---|---|---|---|---|---|---|---|
| Professionally trained judges | Yes | Yes | Yes | Yes | Yes | Yes | Y&N | Y&N |
| Inquisitorial | Yes | Yes | Yes | Yes | Yes | Yes | Yes | No |
| Possibility of informal dialogue with legal system | Yes | Yes | Yes | Yes | Yes | Yes | Yes | No |
| Judge remains with case | Yes | Yes | Yes | Yes | Yes | Yes | some-times | not usually |
| Legal representation for parents usual | No | No | Yes | No | No | No | No | Yes |
| Legal representation for children usual | No | No | No | No | No | No | No | Yes |
| Entry to legal sphere systematically discouraged | Yes | Yes | No | No | No | Yes | Yes | Yes |
| Children's judges work with both juvenile justice and child protection | Yes | Yes | Yes | Yes | Yes | Yes | Yes | No |
| Child's welfare constitutes grounds for intervention | Yes | Yes | Yes | Yes | Yes | Yes | Yes | No |
| Harm and parental responsibility as only grounds for intervention | No | No | No | No | No | No | No | Yes |

KEY:
| | | | |
|---|---|---|---|
| B(FL) | Belgium (Flemish) | I | Italy |
| B(FR) | Belgium (Francophone) | N | Netherlands |
| Fr | France | S | Scotland |
| G | Germany | E | England |

In all other European countries there is some possibility of an *informal dialogue* between the social workers and the judge, or in the case of Scotland, the reporter and the children's panel. In England there is not. In other countries, the families, both parents and children have a possibility of asking to talk to the children's judge. We do not have enough information to know how far this possibility is made use of by children, but it exists, and it is used by parents.

While it is possible for cases in England at the county court and high court level to be kept by the same judge throughout, the *continuity* is not usually possible at the magistrates court level where most cases are heard. The fact that a judge stays with a case from beginning to end, and is expected to review the case at regular intervals creates a different relationship between the judge, the social worker and the family. The judge becomes part of the process of the case and joins in the dialogue in a way that the English magistrates cannot. It makes it more possible and more likely for the discourse of welfare to displace the legal discourse. (King and Piper 1990).

It is common for the *legal representation of parents* to be possible, it is uncommon for it to be systematically used. The adversarial system creates the need for this.

*Legal representation for children* is equally unusual. In several countries there was an interest in the role of the guardian ad litem in representing children's interests, but this was not seen as legal representation.

In some countries, there are barriers set up to discourage the use of the legal system. In both the Belgian communities there are specific organisations within the administrative system aimed at *deflecting cases from the legal system*, and the Scottish reporters can be seen similarly. In the Netherlands, the confidential doctor service in some respects functions as a way of preventing the use of compulsion. In France, Germany and Italy, there is no structural barrier between the social workers and the legal system. England does not have a structural barrier, but does make it very difficult to find the grounds for referral to court, and was therefore included as systematically discouraging entry to the legal sphere.

England is the only country that *separates child welfare and juvenile justice*. This is a difference with very important implications. It is based on a different understanding and philosophy of child development and responsibility, and connected to the English use of the legal rather than the welfare discourse in legal responses to both child protection and children's crime. (Pitts 1995, Downes 1994).

In all the countries studied except for England there was a possibility of judicial *intervention on the basis of the child's welfare alone*. In several countries, recent legislation has tightened up the grounds; the level of information needed for action to be taken and the presentation of the information has been made more formal. They are still a long way from the level of formality required by the family proceedings courts.

In no other country is it necessary to have *evidence of significant harm* related to parental responsibility in order to be able to take other than short term emergency legal action. The effect of this can be seen in Grid 3.

### The administrative sphere of the eight systems

In both Belgian communities, in France and in Scotland, there is an important person or structure in the administrative system, who acts as a *filter between the administrative and legal spheres*. In Belgium, the *conseiller* in the Francophone community, and the mediation committee in the Flemish community, in France the *inspecteur* of *ASE*, in Scotland the reporters, all have a function in channeling cases from the administrative to the legal system. We are not aware of anyone in a similar role in Germany, Italy or the Netherlands. The confidential doctor service in the Netherlands actively avoids referral on to the legal system.

## Figure 2: The administrative sphere of the eight systems

| ADMINISTRATIVE | B(FL) | B(Fr) | Fr | G | I | N | S | E |
|---|---|---|---|---|---|---|---|---|
| Important administrative intermediary figure or system | Yes | Yes | Yes | No | No | No | Yes | No |
| Extensive use of voluntary agencies at all levels | Yes | Yes | No | Yes | No | Yes | No | No |
| Social Services as first port of call | No | No | Yes | No | Yes | No | No | Yes |
| Specialist child protection investigative service | Yes | Yes | Y&N | Y&N | No | Yes | Yes | No |
| Separation of social work task between judicial, child protection and family support | Yes | Yes | Yes | Yes | Yes | Yes | No | No |
| Confidential non-compulsory service | Yes | Yes | No | Yes | No | Yes | No | No |

France, England and Scotland are unusual in the extent to which the services for children and families are *dominated by the local authority social services* departments. In both these countries voluntary agencies exist and play an important part, but there is nothing like the systematic reliance on voluntary agency provision that appears elsewhere in Europe. Italy appears to be in a mid-way position, with extensive reliance on voluntary agencies, but without the same philosophy of subsidiarity as Belgium, Germany and the Netherlands. This difference in the delivery of services creates quite different problems and opportunities in co-operation between agencies.

The result of this difference is that in France, Italy and England, the social services department is likely to be the *first place that a family will be referred to* (or refer itself to) if there are problems. In Scotland there is the alternative with the reporters and the children's panel. The subsidiarity principle increases the possibilities for a family to make choices about the help that they receive, and to make their own definition of their problem.

In Belgium, the Netherlands and Scotland, there is a specialist *service with the function of investigating child abuse*; in Belgium these services also have a wider role, in the Netherlands the child protection board has a largely investigative role. In Scotland the reporters could be seen as having this role, although with a difference. In France there is the possibility for the children's judge to use social services run by the Ministry of Justice, or voluntary agency services working under contract. In Germany, the *Jugendamt* has some role in investigating, and tends to be seen as an investigative service, but has a much wider role, and can also offer support and therapeutic help as well as advice to the court. The Italian social workers did not see investigation as part of the social work task. Several continental social workers expressed surprise at the investigative role of the English local authority social worker. Some of the investigative work undertaken by English social workers would not be undertaken by social workers at all; if it happened, it would be the task of the police, and would be in relation to the possible prosecution of the perpetrator. Other levels of investigative work would not be necessary because there would not be the need to provide evidence of singificant harm.

In other countries there frequently is a separation between the work done with families under a *judicial order* and the work done with families on a *voluntary basis*. This is not a question of voluntary work being done by voluntary agencies. Many judicial supervision orders are carried out by voluntary services in Belgium, France and the Netherlands. But the same family on moving from voluntary to compulsory intervention is likely to change their agency and their social worker.

Three countries have what we have called a *confidential non-compulsory service*. This is something more than the confidential telephone lines, such as Childline, or the respectively blue and green help lines of Italy and France. In the Flemish community of Belgium, the confidential doctor centres provide a therapeutic resource which is specifically intended to provide a confidential service outside the legal and administrative framework of child protection. In Germany the *Kinderschutzdienst* amongst others offers a specialised confidential counselling service for children, adolescents and families. In the Netherlands, the confidential doctor service co-ordinates other agencies and puts families in touch with sources of help, but again only makes referrals with the agreement of the family.

### The use of compulsion — a comparison

In Figure 3 we have logged the responses of different groups to one particular aspect of their thinking on the case. This is discussed further in chapter 9. We wanted to see what the differences were in the stages at which in different countries the social workers thought that it would be appropriate to use compulsion, and at which stages they thought that compulsion was a practical possibility. The rather general word 'compulsion' has been used in order to cover the wide range of differences between the systems of the different countries.

## Figure 3: The use of compulsion in different systems

|                              | B(FL) | B(Fr) | Fr  | G   | I   | N   | S   | E   |
|------------------------------|-------|-------|-----|-----|-----|-----|-----|-----|
| STAGE 1                      |       |       |     |     |     |     |     |     |
| Use of compulsion desired    | No    | No    | No  | No  | No  | No  | No  | No  |
| Use of compulsion possible   | No    | No    | Yes | Yes | Yes | Yes | No  | No  |
| STAGE 2                      |       |       |     |     |     |     |     |     |
| Use of compulsion desired    | No    | No    | Yes | No  | No  | No  | No  | Yes |
| Use of compulsion possible   | Yes   | Yes   | Yes | Yes | No  | Yes | No  | No  |
| STAGE 3                      |       |       |     |     |     |     |     |     |
| Use of compulsion desired    | No    | No    | Yes | No  | Y&N | No  | Yes | Yes |
| Use of compulsion possible   | Yes   | Yes   | Yes | Yes | Yes | Yes | Yes | No  |
| STAGE 4                      |       |       |     |     |     |     |     |     |
| Use of compulsion desired    | No    | No    | Yes | No  | Yes | Yes | Yes | Yes |
| Use of compulsion possible   | Yes   | Yes   | Yes | Yes | Yes | Yes | Yes | No  |

**At stage one** none of the countries wanted to use compulsion; all the social workers were saying that they did not have enough information. In France, Germany and the Netherlands compulsion seemed to be a possibility that could be called on rather more readily then elsewhere, but this did not mean that the social workers had any more wish to use it. Simply, the barriers for the social workers seemed in these countries to be less.

**At stage two** very few social workers wanted to use compulsion, but in France it seemed that the refusal of the parents to co-operate would make the social workers consider the possibility rather more actively. In England, the social workers were anxious and unable to get any evidence which could be potentially used in a court hearing; it seemed as though they would have liked to be able to compel the parents to co-operate as the only way forward. Only Italy, Scotland and England seemed to feel that compulsory action was impossible at this point. England was the only country where there was a conflict between the need to use compulsion to protect the children, and the possibility of doing so.

**At stage 3** the Scottish social workers joined the French and the English in feeling that they were stuck if they could not use compulsion. Only the English at this stage could still see no way of doing so.

**At stage four** the Belgians and the Germans still wanted to work on a voluntary basis and hoped to be able to do so. Elsewhere there was a feeling that the children's needs could now only be met through action that, if necessary, was against the parents' wishes. In all other countries, including Belgium and Germany, this action would by now have been possible. In England, it was now less possible than at the end of stage three.

The ability to use compulsion should not be seen as an indicator that it is necessarily used. For example, in the Netherlands, where it would have been possible to refer the case to the child protection board at stage one, if the social worker thought necessary, the preferred course throughout was to refer, if anywhere, to the confidential doctor service, which would not use any compulsion. The confidential doctor service seemed to provide a way of making it clear to the parents that there were serious concerns outside of a formal framework. In France, the referral of a family to the children's judge can hinge on exactly the lack of co-operation that this case outline describes. Given co-operation, French social workers will work with a high level of risk without seeking court orders. In Italy, by contrast, the social workers were very certain in the first two stages that they could not use compulsion and in the last two stages that they could.

England stands out as being the only country where there was felt to be no possibility of using compulsion even at the final stage, and where the social workers felt so unable to advance without compulsory powers. The child assessment order did not seem to be considered to be usable or effective (possible reasons for this are explored in Chapter 9). The English social workers wished to be able to take authoritative action, but the social work task in England required the collection of evidence, and this was being effectively blocked by the parents' non-co-operation.

# Section Three:
# Important Themes

This section looks in detail at some of the most important themes that arose from our research. Chapter 6 considers the inter-relationship of structure, culture, ideology and the functioning of different systems giving examples from the discussions with social workers in the countries that we studied. Chapter 7 develops the idea that different perspectives give us a different understanding by looking at a specific example, that of child centred practice as understood in different countries. Chapter 8 looks at differences and similarities in social work ideology and practice, and relates this to the cultures and structures within which practice takes place. Chapter 9 analyses the way in which our research participants' view of a particular (hypothetical) case expressed a relationship between the state and the family. This was significantly different in each country and very influential in determining the functioning of the child protection system.

# Chapter 6:
# Understanding difference

The study we have described was concerned to elicit the views of social workers about their own practice in child protection work, and also about the practice of their foreign counterparts. Their comments were thus primarily directed to the social work component of their respective child protection systems. Moreover, it is natural that they should be most preoccupied with the social work aspects of child protection since this is where their experience lies. Thus, the picture to emerge of these systems will naturally tend to be a 'social-work-centric' one.

A caricature of such a tendency is seen in the fable of the blind man who approaches an elephant, feels its trunk, and on the basis of this experience, declares the elephant to be 'like a large snake'. In this he is of course correct, but only partially so. He would better understand the significance of the snake-like trunk — what it is for and how it relates to the rest of the elephant — if he were also aware of the elephant's height and weight, and the way in which these make it difficult for the elephant to bend down to drink. He would then have a better appreciation of the function of the trunk as, for example, a means of bringing water up to the elephant's mouth.

When Italian social workers saw the English social work role as 'authoritarian and controlling', and the Dutch commented that referral to an English social worker unleashes an 'avalanche' of investigative action which could 'set up antagonism', they were both making valid comparisons between the social work role in England and practice in their own countries. But before concluding that the Italian and Dutch child protection systems are necessarily 'better', one needs to consider the place of social work in the system as a whole.

We noted earlier that all of the national systems we studied had certain key elements in common. All countries have procedures and arrangements for:

- investigation and/or surveillance when there is suspicion that children may be at risk of harm;
- provision of help/support to families to minimise such risk. (Primary, secondary and tertiary prevention);
- judicial intervention to protect children (which can lead to either negotiated or 'compulsory' help for the family/child; or removal of a child from its family);
- provision of therapeutic/rehabilitative measures once children have come to harm;
- monitoring the outcome of court decisions; and
- protocols governing communication between professionals who are involved in child welfare.

However, in different countries, responsibility for ensuring the discharge of these functions is differentially distributed amongst the actors within the total system. The English system is characterised by the fact that social service departments carry a central responsibility for the investigative function: preventive work; initiating judicial intervention; providing/managing any measures ordered by the court; and keeping them under review. Social services departments are also the nodal point for all communication between persons/organisations who are concerned with any child in need or at risk. In no other country studied are all these responsibilities quite so centrally located in any part of the system. That they are in England should facilitate the task of ensuring that responses to children in need are consistent and co-ordinated. It also means that responsibility for the resolution of the dilemmas that are inherent in child protection work are disproportionately concentrated in one segment of the system rather than dispersed throughout it. The competing claims of the needs of a child, the rights of a parent and the requirements of the law cannot always be straightforwardly reconciled. The concurrent imperatives of protecting a child whilst working in partnership with parents; of building trust whilst assembling evidence; the balancing of long-term benefit against short-term risk: these are all complex tasks which are subject to different and potentially incompatible priorities. "Phew! It's a big job," exclaimed one Flemish social worker on learning of the range of responsibilities of her English counterparts. It is small wonder that the English research participants found this multi-faceted role anxiety-provoking, and they viewed with a certain envy the less conflict-prone role of some of their continental counterparts whose work did not require them to combine so many functions. Likewise one can understand the reasons for Dutch reactions to the 'avalanche' of counter-productive intervention, and perception of the Italians (who are not charged with investigative duties) that English social workers are 'authoritarian and controlling'.

And yet in the Netherlands and in Italy, indeed in all the countries we studied, investigation and surveillance do take place. In so far as responsibility for this does not fall so exclusively to social workers, it frees them to have a less ambiguous helping role. The focal point for some of the 'difficult' conflict resolution lies elsewhere within the system. In France it is the children's judge who has the task of bestriding the problematic interface between law and welfare, undertaking a far wider function than the judiciary in England. The fact that the children's judges can exercise considerable discretion, both in terms of the procedures they follow and the decisions they can take, does, if anything, place greater rather than lesser stress and onus of responsibility upon them. They are at the point of strain within their system: it is they who must resolve the contradictions between legal and welfare discourses.

In one sense then, one might say that each national child protection system has a tendency towards 'homeostatic' regulation: that within any one country the respective roles of social workers, police, the courts, teachers, doctors, youth workers etc, have a degree of complementarity which ensures that, one way or another, the separate elements of the child protection task are able to be accomplished. On this basis one might question whether it really matters 'who does what' as long as the system as a whole operates effectively and is able to protect children.

Our experience, however, would lead us to believe that the way in which functions are distributed between the various actors within the system does indeed affect the ethos, style and outcomes of child protection work. This is not to say that different patterns of task distribution are the only, or even the main, determinants of what distinguishes one nation's system from another, but that they nonetheless have some significance is illustrated in comments made by some of the Dutch participants in our study. One observed:

"In Holland we have a much greater division of labour (than in England). There is the child protection board which undertakes the initial investigation, then there is the guardian, acting on behalf of the court, who monitors the situation, but help is basically provided by other institutions — either at home or at an after-school centre or whatever. There are many kinds of agency."

The same participant found it 'very contradictory' that, in England the same agency, and often even the same worker, might undertake all these tasks.

A worker from a voluntary agency elaborated:

> "Our system works because she (indicating another member of the discussion group) is the guardian and I'm the worker.... I can play the good guy... When I meet the family they might say (of the guardian) 'she's a bitch'. I don't agree she's a bitch, but I say 'OK, but why don't you and I co-operate? Let's make some progress so that I can write a beautiful report for the guardian to show how well you have done and make the guardian look like a monkey'."

It was further explained that the guardians, in their turn, could 'use the judge', saying to a family: "I didn't make the decision, the judge did, so let's you and I just make the best of it."

To English ears this notion of workers distancing themselves from responsibility for, or identification with, the 'difficult' decisions has a somewhat odd ring. Does not this encourage splitting? The Dutch however, were adamant that it afforded them an effective strategy for forming alliances with families and facilitating co-operative work: that their system 'worked' because of the way it was structured — because different people were able to do different things.

It seems unlikely that the organisational structures and the distribution of welfare/protection tasks within any one national system evolve entirely by chance or mere historical accident. It is more plausible that they are shaped in a way that both reflects and reproduces ideologies and values of the national culture. Such 'shaping' is not necessarily the product of a conscious or calculated process. Culture, as a complex amalgam of beliefs, attitudes and customs, provides a template for, rather than the text of, policy. Its influence is often indirect and, as such, is not necessarily immediately apparent.

At first sight, the participants in our study and the various national systems they represented would all subscribe to a shared philosophy which guided the work they undertake with children and families. However, as we noted in Chapter 5, global principles are capable of differential interpretation in different countries. Also, where two principles are in competition with each other (where, for example there is incompatibility between the needs of a child and the rights of parents), there can be national differences in the weighting given to each imperative and this determines which principle should prevail. Where such culturally determined priorities exist, they not only have potential implications for the formal arrangements by which welfare systems, and roles within them, are structured and organised, but those same priorities will also tend to permeate the ideas and actions of workers within those systems.

This became apparent during a discussion between English and French social workers. The French expressed surprise at the apparent readiness of the English to contemplate placing a child for adoption. They explained the pre-eminent importance that is attached in France to the maintenance of a child's ties with its natural family. The English queried whether it was possible for social workers to place a child for adoption. This was at first denied, but then the French group went into a huddle and conducted a voluble discussion amongst themselves before coming up with a revised answer: "Well, it is actually legally possible, but it is not something which we would normally consider."

If we seek to understand the differences between what happens in one country and what happens in another, the cultural dimension must be taken into account.

The following examples serve to illustrate the different ways in which national cultural characteristics can influence the style and structures of social work practice in child protection.

## Example 1: The impact of subsidiarity in Germany

In Germany value is attached to the notion that the state should devolve responsibility to the lowest levels (the principle of subsidiarity). It is influential in social affairs generally, but particularly in the practice of youth and social work. It implies,

> "...a graded hierarchical order between various associations, asking restraint from big and anonymous unities, thus giving the subsidiaries the authority for assistance and support of smaller ones, which offer a more personal and effective service... Thus the larger community not only relieves itself of its responsibilities, but also strengthens the motivation for self-realisation of the weaker ones and in this way preserves the greatest possible plurality." (Schäfer, 1995 p.53).

Thus it is not just that control over day to day policy is delegated to local social work agencies, with the attendant diversity in local practice, but there is also a greater variety of welfare organisations each with variegated and specialist orientations. The proportion of voluntary agencies is much higher than in the UK. The relative independence and autonomy of this extensive voluntary sector has the effect of freeing each agency to evolve its own priorities, philosophy and methods of working, rather than having to respond to statutory requirements. There are no regulations which stipulate the detail of how joint work with other agencies should be undertaken (as with English child protection conferences) so that social workers have fewer 'audiences' to which they must play. Their more circumscribed role set means that they are able to be insulated from the range and intensity of expectations that are placed upon their English counterparts. One social worker from a voluntary agency said,

"In cases of abuse or ill treatment we are able to spend a long time working with the child without their parents' knowledge. We have sufficient time to build up a relationship of trust and can work together with the child to see how things can best go forward."

The same worker also indicated that when they held a meeting with other agencies to discuss progress in a case, they could choose not to invite the police or the prosecutor if they felt this might lead to inappropriate legal intervention. Another worker spoke of his extreme reluctance to divulge any information given him in confidence by a child.

One consequence of the relative independence which social work agencies enjoy is that they may be operating in ignorance of the role of other agencies who may also be involved. They are thereby deprived of information that might valuably be shared between them. Organisational independence carries with it the risk that the protective welfare net for vulnerable children might contain holes through which they could fall. Recognising this, one German participant commented, "We're protected to work with the child and are able to take time. But what I would like is if, in parallel with this, we could extend networking."

It was noticeable in the group discussions of workers from both Amsterdam and Koblenz that transfer of information across agency boundaries could sometimes be a somewhat contentious issue. After viewing one of these discussions an English worker observed, "...There was clearly conflict in their points of view... Different agencies have different value systems... How much would they really work together?"

In those countries where subsidiarity is a valued tenet of political philosophy, it finds expression in many areas of civil life and shapes the nature of relationships between state, local government, voluntary organisations, communities, families and individual citizens. It is inevitable that social work structures, procedures and styles of working will be correspondingly influenced.

## Example 2: The Italian family

Italy has traditionally attached great importance to 'the family'. Barzini (1964) writes,

> "The first source of power is the family... Within its walls and among its members, the individual finds consolation, help advice, provisions, loans, allies, accomplices... The law, the state and society function only if they do not interfere with the family's supreme interests." (p.190).

Since this was written, family structures in Italy have undergone some change, and one should in any case be cautious about stereotypical generalisations. Nevertheless, the Italian social workers in the study placed a great premium on working consensually with the whole family unit. "In helping the parents you help everyone" one said. Respect for the privacy of the family was evidenced in the constraints the workers felt about passing on information to other agencies without prior permission. To do so was seen as "absolutely incorrect methodologically".

As elsewhere in Europe, the possibility existed for discussion between families, social worker and judge without formal proceedings being invoked. This was seen as useful in resolving any impasse that may have arisen between clients and social workers. The authority of the judge was respected but not used coercively and no undue stigma attached to such informal hearings. The impression given of the judge's role was one of benign paternalism, perhaps mirroring the role of a respected family elder. Although it was recognised that the judge had, and could use formal power, it seemed as if there was mutual recognition that the family would be allowed to retain its independence provided advice given by the judge was heeded — a compact of reciprocal respect. Most social workers found this a constructive process which facilitated continuing work with the family: "A resort to the authority of the judge enables us to find ways of re-establishing a relationship with the family." Although the possibility of invoking 'legal' authority is present, it is more the 'moral' authority conferred on the judge that characterises such meetings.

One worker from southern Italy saw a less positive side to this emphasis upon respecting families' (relative) immunity from intrusion by outside bodies. In her experience this all too easily became patriarchal collusion between the judiciary, the police and the male head of household, and the voice and needs of the weaker members of the family remained submerged:

> "If the family come from an area like mine where there is a culture of family violence, and this is accepted, then you know what the judge would say. They don't want to intervene in family matters. They don't feel they have the right to make that demand."

The possibility that a child's interests may be subjugated to, or subsumed in, those of the whole family is hinted at by Santosuosso (1991). In his handbook on rights, he advises children who have been abused or neglected by their parents thus:

> "The principal difficulty for an effective defence is that, although Italian law acknowledges your many rights, it does not recognise your right to enforce them. Theoretically the right is yours, but the person who exercises it on your behalf is another person, usually the one with parental responsibility for you." (p.542).

Notions about the relationship between the state and the family thus have potential both for the creation of a constructive 'compact' or of counter-productive 'collusion'. Either way it can be seen how a cultural value can affect child protection practice.

## Example 3: Worker/client co-operation

Of all the participants in the study, it was the group of social workers from Bad Doberan (in the former East Germany) who were most sensitised to the impact of culture upon their working lives. They had after all lived and worked under two regimes with dramatically contrasting ideologies. The cultural upheaval they had experienced with the transition from the one system to the other was a frequent and recurring theme in their discussion. Almost every observation they made contained qualifying explanations — "before it was like that, but now it is like this."

Although they currently operate under the same legal framework as their counterparts in the former West Germany, there remain some legacies from former practice. One aspect of this was highlighted when, having viewed the video discussion of the English social workers, they were struck by the way in which there might be no action taken if a family refused to co-operate and there was no evidence of harm to a child:

> "What surprised me was the opinion of one of the (English) social workers who said that she could not actually intervene in

a case because, without the co-operation of the parents, it was not possible to refer the case or to get to grips with it. That disappointed me somewhat... One can't put the problem aside because of lack of co-operation... One has to persevere."

This theme was vigorously supported by his colleagues, one of whom narrated how she had lain in wait for an evasive parent outside a kindergarten: "there are all sorts of ways of getting to see parents." All members of the Bad Doberan group reported that cases where a family refused to co-operate with a social worker were extremely rare. Exploring this theme further the social workers suggested that custom and tradition under their former Communist regime — in particular the relationship between state or community officials and citizens — may have played a part in clients' readiness to co-operate.

"Perhaps this grew out of our historical development a bit. Our people here (in the former DDR) were already accustomed to the idea of people visiting the house... They don't immediately clam up when someone calls. In the former West Germany, and in England too I think, it may be more problematic when people are visited."

Alongside the expectation that the demands of authorities were to be complied with, there was also a sense of communalism in which members of a local community shared a responsibility for each other. It was accepted that communal concern could quite properly override considerations of individual rights and individual privacy. Describing this, Pogge von Strandmann (1994) writes that it was:

"...usual for volunteers and carers to gather information about families and children from teachers, employers and work colleagues and even the *Klassensprecher*, the class prefect. These people could also be invited to give their information to a committee, though the classmate would be expected to leave before decisions were made. This method of enquiring into and looking after a family's or child's affairs was seen by the workers I interviewed as good and caring rather than as an invasion of privacy." (p.6).

However, it is not simply that people were acquiescent and accustomed to the intervention of 'authority' under the former regime, or that personal privacy was seen as subordinate to collective interests. There is also the 'double whammy' effect that the more liberal character of post-unification 'authority' is seen as being helpful, in welcome contrast with what went before, and people are eager to avail themselves of the services available:

> "They can see that it is a very different service that visits them now... during the DDR times the service had great power... whereas now we can offer services. Before there was much fear, but that has changed now."

A colleague added that, after supervision of a child under a court order has been revoked, "most families want this help to continue; they are always saying 'we still need you'."

Clearly a cultural context which, for whatever reason, predisposes clients to work with, rather than evade, social workers will shape the character of child protection work, minimising the necessity for judicial intervention and maximising the possibilities for 'partnership'. Interestingly, this term was not a familiar one to the Bad Doberan participants, but they were very much drawn to it as an apt description of their style of work. They took both pleasure and pride in the new emphasis on 'helping' in their work:

> "What is good about our system is the various forms of help that can be offered. They can be tailored to meet individual need, and this is well received... We have developed a 'landscape' of voluntary services which bring a professional hallmark to service provision and we can be pleased about that."

One participant however, did register a note of reservation:

> "There is another side that is less positive. With the old interventionist authorities there was a tight system which meant that no child could fall through the net. Children were protected."

## Example 4: Individual rights

Box 6 in Chapter 3 drew a distinction between the concepts of 'social rights' and 'individual rights'. The former embodies the notion that there is a broad consensus of interests between individuals, families, communities and the state: that what is good for one is good for the others: all citizens have a right to be part of society and to look for help from it. The reciprocal right of the collective is that individuals will identify themselves with it and make responsible contributions to social life. This conception of rights is more prevalent in continental Europe while the emphasis in Britain is somewhat different. Here, the interests of individuals, families, communities and state are seen as potentially in competition, or even conflict with each other. From this viewpoint it is quite consistent that central government, as the superordinate body, should intervene in a regulatory way to ensure that conflicts of interests are resolved or fought out according to a 'fair' set of rules. The interests of 'fairness', however, also dictate that there should be institutionalised restraints which place some check upon the state's intrusion into the affairs of individual citizens.

This 'double-edged' regulatory role is very evident in the operation of the English child protection system.

Relative to much continental practice, the British system seems to lay more emphasis upon protecting the child *from* the family, as opposed to protecting the child *with* the family. The child's safety takes priority over the needs of the parents or the family unit as a whole. Intervention is first and foremost on the child's behalf. There is an extensive array of arrangements designed for the safeguarding of children:

- the social worker's 'duty to investigate' (Children Act 1989 s47[1]);
- DOH guidelines concerning inter-agency 'intelligence gathering', information sharing and consultation;
- the establishment of joint child protection teams, involving social work/police liaison;
- special procedures for disclosure interviews;
- strategy meetings;
- child protection conferences;
- the child protection register;
- the emergency protection order and the child assessment order;
- the possibility for children to have independent legal representation in court proceedings;
- the possibility of placing a child for adoption if parental consent is 'unreasonably withheld'.

The scope of this repertoire of measures, which surprised and even shocked many continental research participants, reflects the degree to which the state sees itself as responsible for regulating what goes on in families. Although English professionals would not seek to invoke these procedures unnecessarily or oppressively, the measures available to them nonetheless represent considerable incursions into the family domain with a corresponding potential for infringing the rights of parents.

However, parents are not without protection in the English rights-oriented system. In the absence of a court order, they are not obliged to receive a visit from a social worker or to provide them with information. Social workers and/or police cannot initiate any legal proceedings without evidence that a child has suffered, or is at risk of, 'significant harm', and in the absence of parental co-operation, such evidence may be hard to come by. Should a child protection conference be called, parents have a right to be present, to hear what is said about them and to present their own views. Finally of course, no court order can be made unless the court is satisfied with the evidence presented to it.

Arrangements to secure the child's right to protection, and the due process of law protecting parents' rights against arbitrary bureaucratic interference can sometimes have the effect of cancelling each other out. English social workers in our study frequently expressed frustration about this sort of impasse.

Absent from the English system is the relative informality which characterises many of the continental countries: which enables social workers, parents or children to initiate an informal discussion with a judge, to seek advice or negotiate solutions to problems that have arisen. Such arrangements would run counter to the English legal maxim that 'informality breeds illegality'.

The pre-eminent role of the law as protector of individual rights was ever present in the minds of the English social workers' discussion of the hypothetical case. Frequently, any action they contemplated was checked for its legality. When they contemplated the use of authority, it was authority statutorily conferred upon them. The possibility of using their 'professional authority' (i.e. that deriving from their own expertise) was less apparent in their discussions.

This contrasted with the Dutch and Italian groups who echoed comments of the East Germans in stressing that one can and should persevere in attempts to engage with an evasive or unco-operative family, being quite insistent if necessary.

## Discussion of examples

These examples do not do justice to the entirety and complexity of the cultures of the nations referred to. In each case just one aspect of the respective cultures has been isolated for illustrative purposes — offering snapshots rather than a panoramic view. This notwithstanding, they do show how a commonly held belief, perception, attitude or expectation can find expression in the shape and manner of the way that different national systems go about the business of protecting children. What is particularly interesting is that these cultural values are not only reflected in the structures devised to accomplish the child protection task, but also in the minds of the agents within those structures and the recipients of their services. The analogy here is of the bottle in the sea, which at one and the same time is surrounded by, and contains, water.

It is important not to see the impact of culture as simply a linear process in which:

- culturally determined priorities are reflected in legislation, which in turn...
- shapes organisational structures, which in turn...
- impinge upon the nature of the professional task, which in turn...
- lends a particular character to professional intervention, which in turn...
- elicits a particular type of response from service users.

There is a certain logic to this 'top-down' causal chain, and it is certainly true that the more 'powerful' components of a system (e.g. the legislature) are able to exert a disproportionate influence over the less powerful, by defining what is 'important' or 'valuable', and by the ability to enforce compliance to its dictates. However, this is an altogether too simplistic view of how culture operates. To the extent that all actors within a system — legislators, managers, professionals, service users — subscribe to a shared value, then the process by which that value is transmitted and maintained is a more circular one. In the Italian example given above, it is families themselves who assert their independence from state or bureaucratic intrusion. Officials and professionals, who are themselves members of families, uphold the same value and structure their intervention in accordance with it. Similarly, in the example from the former East Germany, it was the attitudes and expectations of citizens that enabled a consensual style of working, which lent a particular character to the style and priorities of professional and judicial intervention. The way in which all parts of a system act in accordance with a shared value has a reciprocally reinforcing effect upon its maintenance.

*This observation underlines the difficulties that would accompany attempts to introduce change to just one part of the system. The surrounding structures of the system, and the mind-set of the participants in it, would also have to change in order to accommodate the new element.*

Lorenz (1996), describing meetings between professionals from different countries, confirms this, but he registers an important qualification:

"Partners always had to operate at two levels; at one level, the national differences, the particular character and requirements of a welfare system rooted in very different political systems and cultures remain deep and unbridgeable... But at another level, the contacts showed that social pedagogues and social workers could work together very well, that staff in child protection in different countries under different systems shared common principles and concerns..." (p.27).

In this connection it is interesting to note that in the examples given above of (German) subsidiarity, the (Italian) attitude to the family and (former East German) co-operative nature of worker-client relationships, three quite different cultural characteristics appear to contribute to very similar consequences. In all three cases, cultural features operate to enhance the possibility that child protection problems can be resolved through informal negotiation rather than judicial compulsion (Figure 4 below summarises in chart form the routes by which this occurs). So, from different starting points, professionals are undertaking a very similar style of work. Equally, in all three cases, representatives from within each respective system noted that there may be a price to pay for this, namely the risk that abuse of children may remain unnoticed or unattended to. Any coin, however valuable, has its 'reverse side', and the tension that this creates provides impetus and incentive for a system to countenance change, as opposed to remaining locked within traditional ideas and approaches.

*Different cultural characteristics are not necessarily incompatible with each other just because they are different. Values inherent in one can nonetheless exist in another. Barriers to cross-cultural influences are thus not absolute.*

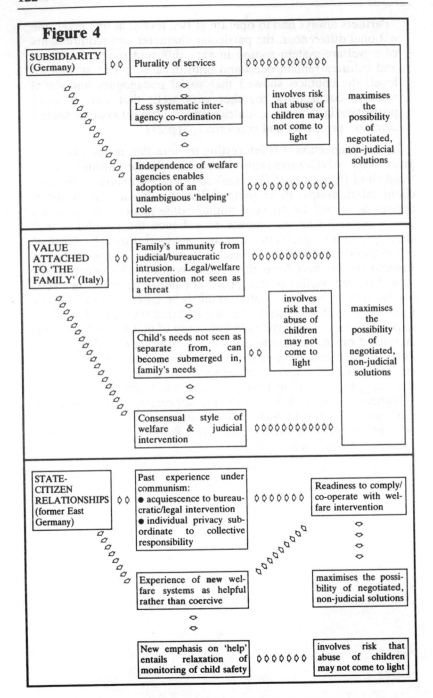

**Figure 4**

| SUBSIDIARITY (Germany) | Plurality of services | | involves risk that abuse of children may not come to light | maximises the possibility of negotiated, non-judicial solutions |
| | Less systematic inter-agency co-ordination | | | |
| | Independence of welfare agencies enables adoption of an unambiguous 'helping' role | | | |

| VALUE ATTACHED TO 'THE FAMILY' (Italy) | Family's immunity from judicial/bureaucratic intrusion. Legal/welfare intervention not seen as a threat | | involves risk that abuse of children may not come to light | maximises the possibility of negotiated, non-judicial solutions |
| | Child's needs not seen as separate from, can become submerged in, family's needs | | | |
| | Consensual style of welfare & judicial intervention | | | |

| STATE-CITIZEN RELATIONSHIPS (former East Germany) | Past experience under communism:<br>• acquiescence to bureaucratic/legal intervention<br>• individual privacy subordinate to collective responsibility | | Readiness to comply/co-operate with welfare intervention | |
| | Experience of **new** welfare systems as helpful rather than coercive | | maximises the possibility of negotiated, non-judicial solutions | |
| | New emphasis on 'help' entails relaxation of monitoring of child safety | | involves risk that abuse of children may not come to light | |

## Learning from difference

Consideration of culturally determined differences between national child protection systems leads one into a quagmire of conundrums and apparent contradictions. In comparing one with another one is confronted by:

- things that look the same, but which on closer inspection are not;

  *e.g. In all of the countries involved in our study, social workers were of the firm opinion that the best place for a child was in its own natural family. However, opinions about the point at which a child may have to be removed from its family were by no means universally shared.*

- things which look different, but which on closer inspection are not;

  *e.g. The English system is unique in the stress and anxiety that it lays upon those charged with implementing it. Not so: social workers in the English system do indeed have to reconcile problematic and contradictory legal and welfare imperatives, but this same stress can still be present in other systems, merely located elsewhere within it — e.g. the French children's judge.*

These need to be distinguished from:

- things which look, and really are, the same;

  *e.g. The commitment of social workers in all of the countries studied that their intervention should be directed towards the independence and autonomy of their clients.*

- things which look, and really are, different;

  *e.g. The controlling role of central government in Britain as opposed to, say, Germany or Holland where the subsidiarity principle places limits upon the scope of central government involvement.*

The ability to make these distinctions has implications both for understanding and learning from other countries. It is tempting to look to other countries with an eye for good ideas or innovatory practice. But to wander round the 'European supermarket' filling one's trolley with a bit of subsidiarity here and a confidential doctor there is a somewhat futile exercise. Practices rooted in one particular cultural context cannot so easily be uprooted for transplantation into another unless the importing culture and structures are able to make the substantial adjustments necessary to accommodate it.

The experience of the Bad Doberan social workers is interesting in this respect. After German reunification they did indeed experience the importation of new ways of working, but in their case they were not so much incorporating a single new idea as acquiring a whole new system complete with ideology and organisational structures. Adjustment to such massive changes must have been traumatic, but they were possible precisely because the changes were so comprehensive. It was not a case of new patches being sewn onto old material.

If then, one discounts the 'supermarket' model of looking at the practices of other countries, does this limit us to to a 'theme park' approach — where all we can do is gaze, find it all very interesting, but not expect to take the exhibits home with us? This seems an altogether too pessimistic view. We have elsewhere in this book elaborated upon the potential value of exposure to foreign practice as a means of stimulating critical reflection on one's own domestic practice. Over and beyond this, the notion that 'culture' is so powerful and pervasive that it will necessarily and always inhibit the introduction of new ideas from without is not totally sustainable. National culture is not immutable; it can and does shift, accommodate and evolve. European cultures, despite their differences, have much in common, and as economic and political ties are strengthened it is likely that national ideologies will become more permeable. As Lorenz (1996) suggests,

> "Experience... has shown that once issues get related very closely to practice and the development of action programmes and skills, the conceptual barriers will not be insurmountable." (p.28).

There is much about European practice that, while it may be 'different', is nonetheless culturally congruent and can highlight themes and principles which are capable of inspiring and enriching the domestic debate about future developments in child care practice.

Quite apart from this, to realise that elsewhere things are done differently, expands one's confidence in the belief that 'different things' *can* be done. To adapt an observation of H. G. Wells' Mr Polly, "Once you have seen through the paper walls of everyday circumstance, those insubstantial walls that hold us so securely... you can change..." (p.156).

# Chapter 7:
# Children — objects or subjects?

One of the recommendations put forward by Dame Butler-Sloss in the Cleveland report (Butler-Sloss, 1988) was that the child should be treated as a person and not as 'an object of concern'. How far has this been achieved, and if it has not, what is preventing its achievement? It is, after all, a proposition with which social workers would readily agree. The emphasis of the Children Act 1989 on the primacy of the child's interest has had the whole-hearted and active endorsement of the social work profession.

As has already been indicated, social workers in all the countries we worked with had similar concerns. They all saw the child as the most important person in any situation, and they all saw the child's interest as paramount. However, they were working in situations where the laws were different, the expectations about families were different, and where there were different ideas about the relationship between children and power. How might this affect their understanding of the way that they worked with children and what they actually did?

In attempting child-centred practice, there are three external constraints on a practitioner. These constraints derive in part from specific legislation but also from accepted behaviour and popular expectation. The three areas to consider are:

- *the right to confidentiality*; what confidentiality can a child expect, and under what circumstances? Does this vary according to age, and if so what are the relevant ages?
- *the right to be interviewed/counselled*; can a child be interviewed or counselled without parental permission, or without parental knowledge? If so, do there have to be grounds that

make this possible, and what are they?

• *the right to refuse help*; does a child who is being abused have the right to refuse help? Who, if anyone can override that right? On what grounds?

All the systems studied show different combinations of responses to these questions, but for the purposes of this discussion, they can be considered in three broad groups: the northern continental group made up of Belgium, the Netherlands and Germany; the southern continental group made up of France and Italy; and the off-shore island group made up of Scotland and England. It is important to remember the countries we did not study. Many of them would have fallen geographically in the southern continental group or in the off-shore island group, and we studied no Scandinavian countries. The grouping used here is purely for convenience and does not claim to be making a definition. That being said, this grouping makes certain patterns of child-centred practice more visible.

## Child-centred work with a pre-school child

We gained information about the social workers' approach to working with children from the hypothetical case. The story describes a situation involving two children, Andrew aged four and his older sister Frances, aged 13. (For a full version see Chapter 6.) Andrew was at a playgroup (in some countries, a nursery school, depending on what was the norm for the country in question). At the second stage of the case, his teacher reported to the head of the establishment that Andrew's attendance was poor and that he was aggressive to other children. How did the social workers react to this information about a four year old, and what action did it lead to?

## The northern continental group

In all countries the social workers took this very seriously. They saw Andrew's behaviour as reflecting his experience at home. Most workers made a very explicit connection between aggressiveness to other children and either a direct experience of violence, or the witnessing of violence. In the Flemish community of **Belgium**, the aim was to take matters further without legal intervention. While still working on a voluntary basis, various services were suggested such as school psychological services, or persuading the family to go to a family centre. Some of the workers thought that the situation was serious enough to consider referring the family to the confidential doctor service or the committee for special youth assistance because they saw Andrew's behaviour as 'sending a signal'.

In the Francophone community of Belgium, the response was rather similar. Andrew's behaviour was seen as a sign of family dysfunction, and they would consider, if they could not get the co-operation of the parents, a referral to the *Service Aide à la Jeunesse*, or to the *conseiller*. This would still be within the administrative part of the system, but would begin to bring the family within an official orbit. For the Belgian social workers from both communities, there was the possibility of a referral which would send a clear message to the parents that Andrew's behaviour was considered to be a serious problem, and it would, in practice, be possible for them to see Andrew without parental permission.

The social workers in **the Netherlands** were particularly insistent that they 'would not take no for an answer' from the parents because they considered that it was always possible to make contact with a family if you tried hard enough and thought carefully enough about your approach. They were very concerned about Andrew and would aim to gain his mother's trust in planning ways of helping him. They would be active in involving other agencies to support their work with the family, and they would expect Andrew's teacher to keep in regular telephone contact with them. If the parents would not co-operate, the confidential doctor service, or the child protection board were possible sources of further pressure, without involving referral to the legal system. In all these three systems, being child-centred gave you the right to make demands on parents and on other agencies.

In **Germany**, it would be possible, and this was suggested by most of the workers, to work with Andrew without asking his parents' permission and without their knowledge. It was acknowledged that they might not gain much information from Andrew, but that would not be the main aim. The main aim would be to help him. They would combine intervention with Andrew with other strategies, such as working with the school to help them to support the mother, and offering the mother advice about other agencies to approach, or confidential discussion of the situation. They would call a helpers' conference which would include the nursery, the elder child's school, the *Kinderschutzdienst* and possibly the *Jugendamt* in an advisory capacity, and they would not need to inform the parents of this.

## The southern continental group

For the **French** social workers, there was the possibility of referral at an early stage to the judge for children, and Andrew's behaviour was a major factor in this. The combination of his suffering and the non-co-operation of his parents would have given them grounds. The main purpose in a referral would be to respond to Andrew's distress. The social workers would have preferred to work on a voluntary basis, and still expected to be able to do so, but they saw the intervention of the judge for children as potentially beneficial for the family, and therefore helpful for Andrew. If the social workers were having difficulty in working with Andrew's parents, judicial referral could be a sensible strategy. There was no mention of any difficulty about seeing Andrew.

The **Italian** social workers shared the view of other social workers that Andrew's behaviour was a cry for help and symptomatic of the problems in the family. They were, however, very dependent on being able to engage the family. They could not see Andrew without his parents' knowledge and consent. They considered that the nursery school should be working with this situation, probably involving the school psychologist, but as there was no obligation for a child to attend nursery school, non-attendance could not be made an issue. Some of the workers considered involving the judge for children, either in an informal consultation, or in a formal capacity, in order to give authority to their attempts to engage the family. They saw themselves as agents in helping the family to change, and although concern for Andrew was high, they had no authority to intervene unless the judge for children was involved in some way. The focus of their concern was a need to understand the family enough to be able to think out a plan of work which would engage the family as a whole, and work with the problems of the family as a whole.

## The off-shore island group

In **Scotland**, the social workers were concerned about Andrew's psychological and social development and the focus was on his needs. They saw his behaviour as demonstrating that the family as a whole were in difficulties, and wanted to get a clearer understanding of the family dynamics, but this was secondary to the consideration of his individual needs. As in other countries, they expected to involve the nursery school, and considered various therapeutic possibilities for helping Andrew. There was an expectation that it would be possible with persistence to engage the family, and there was little suggestion of compulsory intervention. Getting to see Andrew was not mentioned as a problem.

The **English** social workers wanted to do a thorough assessment, but said explicitly that they could not speak to either of the children without the parents' permission. They could get further information from the nursery school and the health visitor, but without parental co-operation, they did not have a way forward. There was not felt to be enough evidence for calling a child protection conference, which would be one way of putting pressure on the parents. In two groups the possibility of using a child assessment order was raised, but there was uncertainty as to whether this would be either legally possible or useful, as Andrew was too young to give them information. They needed information in order to be able to act because they had to have evidence. Help for Andrew himself was at this point impossible without parental co-operation. Some social workers thought that ultimately they would be able to get this, but a number thought that they would not be allowed enough time to get through to the parents; the case would not be allocated.

Faced with the hypothetical situation of a young child showing distress through aggressive behaviour, the social workers in the different countries seemed to use much the same frameworks of understanding, but their approach was not the same. They were enabled or constricted both by the legal structures that they worked to, and their view of their role. The focus on the child was there in all countries, but differently in each country, sometimes considerably so.

## Child-centred work with a young adolescent

Andrew's elder sister Frances is 13. Anxieties are raised about her at the first stage of the case, but she comes to the forefront later, when, two weeks after Andrew was referred, her teacher contacts the social worker to say that Frances has run away from home for three days, and, now that she has returned, would like to talk to a social worker. She talks of violence at home, but not towards herself, and hints at possible sexual abuse by her step-father. In all countries, the first reaction of the social workers was to want to meet Frances and establish a trusting relationship with her, so that she could talk to them about what was happening to her. However the context in which the workers would be relating to Frances was not the same everywhere.

## The northern continental group

In **Belgium**, the Flemish and the Francophone social workers wanted to establish a relationship of trust with Frances, and worked within similar contexts. They would be able to see Frances without her parents' knowledge, and they would be able to give her considerable control over what happened. They saw it as important to give her confidence that she could be protected, that her mother and brother could also be protected and that she would not be blamed. They wanted to give her the knowledge about what she could do to protect herself. In the two communities, there are structural and legal differences that affect the detail of the social workers' recommendations, but the approach to Frances was the same in both. She could decide what the next action should be, and they have to gain her trust in order to help her make a decision that would protect her. In both communities, referral to the confidential doctor service (or its equivalent, *SOS Enfance*), the administrative child protection system or to the legal system were possibilities, but the action of the social workers depended considerably on Frances' wishes.

In **the Netherlands**, the social workers had similar aims and a similar context. They emphasised the necessity of creating a relationship with Frances, arranging to meet her on neutral ground, giving her a choice of where they met, and letting her know that if she wished to leave home they would support her. They could find a placement for her if it was not safe at home, and they could ask for legal protection for her. Frances would have the option of confidential counselling through the youth advisory service, or she could ask for legal protection, which would involve an investigation through the child protection board. If she felt unable to make a decision, and they felt it to be necessary, the social workers would decide for her, but Frances had room to make her own decision. While the social workers thought that there was a possibility that the children were in danger, and had reviewed possible emergency action, they thought that at the moment it was more important to work with Frances than to intervene, and they expected to be able to do this.

In **Germany**, there is an explicit legal right to be able to counsel a child without the knowledge of her parents if this is in the child's best interests. (It was this that enabled them to talk to Andrew earlier on in the case.) It would also be possible, up to a point, for Frances to refuse help, or to determine the kind of help that she would accept. (If there is a situation of acute danger, the social worker could overrule her wishes.) The social workers felt certain that Frances was asking for help through her actions, but what kind of help was not clear. They needed to work with her to offer her support and tell her about the possible courses of action that she could take. There would be the possibility of immediate protection in a safe house for young people. If there was less urgency, but she wanted to leave home against her parents' wishes, they would have to involve the legal system; but Frances would have control over whether any of this happened. She could also be asked if she wanted her step-father to be prosecuted, and if she did not, this would be taken seriously.

Frances would have had a great deal of power in the situation, and part of the work with her would have been to create a safe context that would enable her to share this age-inappropriate responsibility. The social workers agreed that there were limitations to a child-centred approach.

> "If it is clear that the child is being abused, and the child says 'I want to stay at home', then the child-centred stance is over. I can no longer say 'the child must decide'. As an adult I must say 'we will decide what must be done, even if it is against your will'."

## The southern continental group

The **French** social workers would nearly all at this point refer the case to the judge for children. They were very concerned to establish a relationship of trust with Frances, to let her know that she was not to blame and to let her know of the ways in which she could be protected. Referral to the judge was seen as a positive step, and the audience with the judge was seen as something that could be supportive for Frances. She could talk to him on her own, and the referral would convey the seriousness of the situation to her parents. The authority of the judge was protective but not accusatory. The social workers also considered the provision of out of school opportunities and activities to improve the quality of Frances' daily life and normalise her experience. There was no conflict for the social workers between the use of statutory authority and a therapeutic intervention, and the referral to the judge did not depend on gathering any further information. This left the social workers free to concentrate on Frances, her needs and her well-being. Frances herself did not have control of what happened next, but judicial referral was seen as an opportunity for her to influence what happens.

In **Italy** the response of the social workers was in some ways similar to that in France, but it was more difficult for them to intervene. They saw their interventions more consistently in terms of intervention with the family as the means of helping the children. They still wanted to work with Frances and establish a relationship of trust with her, but the aim was a more general one of understanding the dynamics of the family, and there was less direct reference to the likelihood of sexual abuse. As in France, if Frances remained at home, several workers thought that she should be offered resources and strategies, such as membership of a youth club to improve her 'insertion' into the school and to improve her social life. As in France, referral to the judge was not only about enabling legal protective measures to be taken, but about using the authority of the judge to enable the social worker to make a relationship with the parents. The judge however, was not described as offering confidentiality or support to Frances.

## The off-shore islands group

The **Scottish** and the **English** social workers shared the same approach and many of the same dilemmas over their work with Frances. They wanted to establish a trusting relationship, and this was clearly linked to getting information about possible sexual abuse. Information would also be important for helping them to understand the family better, but the possibility of sexual abuse raised particular dilemmas for the social workers. They had to make it clear to Frances that if she did disclose abuse, the procedural sequence of child protection conference, disclosure interview and child protection investigation would have to follow, and that what she told them could not be confidential. At the same time, the only way that they could help her, would be by getting her to trust them, and tell them what has been happening.

In both countries, the social workers were uneasy about interviewing Frances without her parents' knowledge, and were concerned about the rights of the parents. In Scotland, nearly all the workers thought at this stage that a referral to the reporter was necessary and possible. In England, the workers referred to a wide range of possible statutory interventions, but always with the proviso that they needed more information. Unless the parents began to co-operate or Frances gave them information which provided evidence of abuse, they were stuck. It was very difficult for them, in good faith to offer a trusting relationship to Frances, and they were very aware of this.

## Confidentiality and the right to counselling

In the northern continental group, there is a high level of

confidentiality possible for a teenager. In the Netherlands this is codified as being 12, because 12 to 25 is the age range covered by the youth advisory centres, and at 13 Frances seems to be accepted in as being old enough to be offered this confidentiality in Belgium in both communities. In Germany, there are a number of organisations that will offer confidential counselling to Frances, although there is some variation about the handling of confidentiality. One agency was absolute; when faced with a case conference, they would not attend because they would not be able to contribute. Another, with a specific child protection focus would be less circumscribed, but would still expect to maintain confidentiality. The *Jugendamt*, which works with the judge for children, was under slightly more pressure, but seemed to be in a similar position.

The right to see a professional without the parents' knowledge is a closely linked issue to that of confidentiality. The clearest position is in Germany, where that right is stated in Paragraph 8 Section 3 of the Child and Youth Welfare Act. (KJHG 1990)

"Children and young people can be counselled without the knowledge of their guardians if the counselling concerns an emergency or conflict situation, and if the aim of the consultation would be undermined by informing the guardian". (KJHG 1990) This has no age barrier, and applied equally to Andrew and to Frances. In the Netherlands, the position of the youth advisory centres in offering confidentiality includes the ability to offer this without informing the parent or guardian. In Belgium the situation was less clearly defined administratively and legally, but the possibility seemed to be there. None of the social workers suggested that there were any difficulties about seeing Frances, although there was slightly less certainty about seeing Andrew. One way of achieving this for the Francophone workers would be for Andrew to be seen by the doctor attached to the nursery school, as this is legally acceptable. The doctor worked in the same building as the social worker, and communication about the family would be easy. The legal position was unclear, but it was felt to be acceptable practice. For workers in the confidential doctor service or *SOS Enfance*, their agency policy of confidentiality made it possible for them to see Frances because she could take the initiative, but harder to see Andrew.

In all four systems in the northern continental group, it was possible for Frances to talk to the social workers and to refuse help. In all four systems there was the possibility of emergency action and legal intervention, but in the situation described, the workers envisaged being able to give Frances control over what happened next. They saw it as their professional responsibility to work with her to gain her trust not only so that she could tell them what was happening, but so that she could trust them enough to take their advice and to let them protect her.

In the southern continental group, there are considerable differences between France and Italy, but similarities in relation to the initial power of the parents, and in the consequent use of the judge for children to overcome this. In Italy a young child could not be seen by the social workers without his parents' permission. (It would be more likely that Andrew would have been seen by the school psychologist, and this would be acceptable within the context of the school). It seemed to be possible to see a teenager, but no institutional system or agency which offered face-to-face confidential counselling to teenagers was referred to at any point. The source of confidential help which could withstand the power of the family would be the judge for children, who could, as in France be approached by the child. The social workers were constricted in what they could do, and their approach was very family centred. Lacking authority themselves, they had to use the authority of the law, the symbolic authority of the judge, to engage the parents. Only the law could intervene in the family for the child as a separate individual. In France it was easy to refer a case to the judge for children, and the social workers' use of the law was similar.

There was however a difference between the French and Italian social workers in their attitude to the rights of the parents and the power of the professionals. The French workers mentioned no problem seeing Andrew or Frances without their parents' knowledge, and expected to be able to work confidentially with Frances. There was not an either/or feeling about their plans. They would work with Frances, both over her own feelings and wishes, and over her social and educational development, they would also refer the case to the judge for children in order to engage the parents. In both France and Italy, the right of a child to refuse help was not specifically considered; the readiness to refer the case to the judge, although slightly different in implications between the two countries, diminished the possibility of the child having control over the unfolding of events. Within the court process, however, the child would have her own space, the judge could see her on her own, and the *audience* could be seen as empowering. By bringing the judicial process into the work at an earlier stage, the possibility of controlling what happens passed from both child and social worker to judge, but the judge was expected to represent the child.

In England and in Scotland social workers were presented with a major dilemma. It is allowed under the Children Act 1989 to accommodate a child of 16 against parental wishes, which implies that at 16 a young person can be offered counselling without parental knowledge. In the hypothetical case, where Frances was 13, the social workers did not feel sure they had the right to work with her or interview her without her parents' knowledge. Several workers referred to the concept of 'Gillick competency' (Cullen, D. 1986, Gillick v West Norfolk and Wisbech Area Health Authority [1986] AC 112), but this did not seem to provide a solution. The whole ethos of their work (as in other countries) was that clients should be offered confidentiality, and should be able to trust social workers. But even if they felt able to intervene, they could not be sure that they could treat what a young person said confidentially. The first thing they had to do was warn her that what she said might have to be told to other people. They had to warn her that she might lose all control over what happened to her and her family. It is not simply that there were procedures that had to be followed, but that the duty to protect a child is so strongly felt that it becomes the overriding responsibility.

The Scottish and English social workers therefore had a limited ability to see a child or young person without their parents' knowledge, had a limited ability to offer confidentiality, and very little ability to give the child or young person any control over what happened next. The Scottish social workers had the resource of referral to the reporter, which gave them the possibility of involving a source of authority, but they were in as much difficulty as the English social workers when they want to see the child, preserve confidentiality or give the child any control over events.

The hypothetical case was useful in clarifying the differences between systems, but it is in hearing about real situations that the impact of these differences is most strongly felt. A German social worker described work with Maria, who was 12. The social worker from the *Jugendamt* was telephoned by one of her clients who said that she had her young sister-in-law with her in distress. Maria was persuaded to talk to the social worker on the telephone and then to agree that the social worker should come round. She agreed on the understanding that nothing further would happen if she did not want it to. The social worker went to her client's flat and there met with Maria, who told her about sexual and physical abuse from her father over a considerable period. Maria was terrified that her father would find out that she had told someone, and would kill her. With Maria's agreement, the social worker rang the police to find out whether they would be able to arrest Maria's father on the

information she had given (which involved other children as well
as herself); the social worker did not tell the police who she was
talking about, or Maria would not have agreed to her contacting
them. The police thought that they would be able to arrest the
father and protect Maria, and on that basis, the social worker
persuaded Maria to go with her to the *Jugendamt*. There they met
the police, and Maria made a statement that enabled the police to
arrest her father.

The social worker was definite that if Maria had not agreed to
talk to her, or to talk to the police, she would not, at that point,
have acted against her wishes. She would have continued to work
with Maria, and expected that with perseverance, she would be
able to gain Maria's confidence enough to be able to take action.
This situation is interesting because not only the social worker but
also the police accept that it is right to allow Maria to have some
control over what happens and when. This goes much further than
the agreement which can be reached in England at strategy
meetings, not to proceed too quickly. Maria was quite clear that
she was currently being physically and sexually abused. English
social workers who heard that story felt that they would not have
been able to work in the same way (Cooper *et al.*, 1996). This
approach is not confined to social workers and the police. In
another German case story, a judge for children refused to make a
compulsory placement order on a family with several children who
were being abused because the children did not want it. At a later
stage when they agreed to the placement, the order was made. On
this occasion, the social worker had been asking for a placement
order. Case material from Belgium described in Chapter 1 shows a
similar empowerment of the child.

The fact that social workers are not expected or not allowed to
give evidence in child abuse cases, and the different approach to
evidence and information in general (see Ely and Stanley, 1990,
Cooper *et al.*, 1995), is an important influence on social work
practice, particularly in relation to sexual abuse. Social workers in
all the continental countries that we studied were not constrained
by the need to avoid contaminating evidence. One 13 year old
French girl, Dorothee, who was living with her aunt, was on a
judicial supervision order. She had previously (while living at
home) made a suicide attempt, and there was a suspicion that she
had been sexually abused, but she had never told anyone directly.
After some months of work with Dorothee, her social worker
asked her whether she had been sexually abused, and she
gradually told him about it. She had been abused by an uncle, who
lived with her parents. With her social worker's support, she was

able to talk to her parents about this for the first time, and they believed her. The parents decided to prosecute her abuser, which was extremely important to her in confirming that they supported her and took it seriously. An English social worker who heard about this work was certain that she could not have initiated the discussion about abuse without being, at the very least, heavily criticised for making prosecution of the offender impossible, and rendering Dorothee's evidence invalid and useless. The French social worker had the authority of the judge for children to work with Dorothee, and could pursue a therapeutically focused course of action without being distracted by other considerations.

In the northern continental countries social workers have a mandate to work with children in ways that could be seen as conflicting with parental rights, and in ways that could be seen as putting the child at risk. They try to avoid referral to the legal system, and they are expected to work with personal professional authority to achieve a result that is safe for the child while respecting her autonomy. In the southern continental countries, where the recourse to the legal system is seen rather differently, there is, particularly in Italy, a stronger sense of the right of the parents to control what happens. However, the legal system can be readily evoked if there is no co-operation from parents, so that the authority of the law is used in getting parental co-operation and safeguarding the child. In all the continental countries, the ready use of judicial supervision orders gives the social workers the delegated authority of the judge in their dealings with parents, which facilitates their access to children.

In a comparable English case involving a girl of 13, it was very hard for the social worker to give her any control at all over what happened. Josie told her teacher that she was worried by the way her mother's boyfriend behaved to her. She did not give much detail, but was distressed and said that his behaviour made her uncomfortable. Following the correct procedures, the teacher told the head teacher, who referred the situation to social services. There followed interviews with Josie and her mother, a videoed disclosure interview and medical examination, strategy meetings, child protection conferences and court hearings. The boyfriend agreed to move out, and finally a supervision order was made to support Josie's mother in protecting Josie. The process of reaching this point was very distressing for Josie, and left her feeling angry and powerless. In spite of the social worker's efforts to work with Josie, (and she provided Josie with a range of resources which were helpful to her), the focus of the process was not Josie but her mother and mother's boyfriend.

The proceduralisation of the English system clearly plays a part in 'objectifying' the child. It is linked to a preoccupation with risk that was remarked on by other social workers. The English social workers were aware of the effects of procedures, and saw them as a potential impediment to good practice.

> "Child protection procedures are streamlined the moment there is an allegation... once you get involved in this (English) system you have to come out doing things whether you like it or not. We seem to be locked into a system whereby preventing abuse, that particular kind of abuse to that particular individual is the overriding factor, when we all know that...abused children have enormous affection towards the abuser...I feel quite uptight about it because, yes, you do stop the abuse, ... and then we all disappear off to do the next case."

This social worker is describing something similar to the process described by Robert Castel in relation to risk in psychiatric medicine:

> "The new strategies dissolve the notion of a *subject* or a concrete individual, and put in its place a number of *factors*, the factors of risk... The essential component of intervention no longer takes the form of the direct face-to-face relationship between the carer and the cared, the helper and the helped, the professional and the client." (Castel, 1991 p.281).

Although this was written about the mental health field, it quite accurately describes the way in which child care social workers in England feel they have become investigators and case managers, with the face-to-face work with parents and children delegated to family aides, family workers, independent play therapists etc. Castel goes on to describe the way in which abstractly calculated *risk* factors take on a predictive role and replace the specific and incident focused concept of *dangerousness*. The words he uses are familiar in the field of child protection; where ten years ago Dale wrote of work with 'dangerous families' (Dale *et al.*, 1986), social workers now do 'risk assessments'. The lesser pre-occupation of social workers in other countries with procedures, risk and evidence makes it easier for them, whatever their view of the place of the child in the family, to keep the child as the subject and not the object of their concerns.

An extremely complex constellation of value positions lies behind all child welfare practice. For Britain, Fox Harding has described and categorised different value positions or mind sets with which child welfare can be approached, drawing on American and British sources (Fox Harding, 1991). She defines four categories, laissez-faire and patriarchy, state paternalism and child protection, the modern defence of the birth family and parents' rights, and children's rights and children's liberation. This is a detailed and convincing exploration of the values which influence British social work in child welfare, and the constellations in which these values appear. The problem in learning about the practice of another country is that even though the same values may be present, the patterns and constellations of values are different. The French system accommodates the 'parents' rights' and the 'state paternalism' without the conflict between them that Fox Harding describes; in Germany and Holland, 'state paternalism' seemed to be co-existing with 'children's rights and children's liberation'.

English social workers see themselves as child centred; but there are conflicts for them in achieving this, conflicts between child-centred practice and parental rights, and between child-centred practice and child rescue. To the English, the continental social workers were on the one hand very high-handed about parents' rights, and on the other hand, over ready to take risks with children's safety. Some English social workers with whom we have discussed these cases felt that the readiness of French, Belgian and German social workers to let children return home to potentially abusive situations was dangerous and unprofessional. Conversely, some saw it as an empowerment of the children for them to be allowed to make their own decisions about risk and about what was most important to them. The different reactions emphasise the very strong child rescue ethos of work with children and families in England and Scotland and the conflicts that this can create over children's rights.

If a primary value is put on the safety of the child and the prosecution of the perpetrator, then the English system makes sense. Meeting these objectives however, gets in the way of meeting other objectives, such as listening to the child's priorities, offering confidentiality to the child, building a trusting and therapeutic relationship with the child or building the child's confidence and self-esteem through their own positive action. As Fox Harding demonstrates, the child's interest can be interpreted in many different ways, so that giving primacy to the child's interests does not necessarily avoid treating the child as an 'object of concern'. An imperative both to respect parental rights and avoid risk creates formidable barriers to the treatment of the child as a person.

# Chapter 8:
# The social work task in context

The seventies and eighties sparked off several important debates on how children should be cared for and protected, not only in Britain but in continental Europe and the United States, where concepts such as the 'best interest of the child', (Goldstein, J. *et al.*, 1973) and the debates leading up to the UN charter on children's rights in 1989, brought a gradual realisation that children should not only be considered in the context of politics and policies for the family as a whole, but that they should become 'subjects' rather than 'objects' of policies and politics in their own right (see Chapter 7). In England the Children Act 1989 embodied much of the new thinking of the preceding years as did new child care legislation in other countries, such as Belgium, Scotland, France and Germany, where debates similar to those in England were conducted. What does not seem to have happened to the same extent in other countries as in England are public enquiries into cases of child abuse, where social workers and the social work profession were subjected to public scrutiny and criticism. This difference and its consequences were starkly demonstrated at an NSPCC seminar where social workers from those countries who had participated in the comparative study and who had been invited to attend commented that "the first question we were asked by English social workers and administrators in our group discussions, was: how many children died in your country as a result of child abuse?" (Cooper *et al.*, 1996). The surprise about this question, which was asked of all the participants from abroad in their various groups, was linked to the assumption that this question should be relevant to their work. They were in the business of preventive and interventive work for children and families, they worked in voluntary and statutory agencies, but they did not see themselves directly or solely accountable for child deaths.

The child abuse enquiries, however, focused not only on social workers but also on child protection systems and how these could be improved. The Children Act 1989 introduced the principle of the 'best interest of the child' as a primary consideration together with the concept of the 'child in need' which included children with disabilities and provisions to help children and families in need. New child care legislation in other European countries such as Scotland, Belgium, Holland, France and Germany reflect concerns with the rights of the child, the importance of listening to the child's voice and the shared responsibility between the state and the parents to care for children. The *Kinderjugendhilfegesetz* (KJHG) or Children and Youth Services Act (1990) in Germany and the Youth Assistance Act (1990) in Flanders are, perhaps, most radical in focusing primarily on the provision of preventive help and assistance on a broad scale, especially educative or pedagogical help which is to be provided to children and young people in their families and in their communities rather than in institutions. The rationale for these measures and for the financial expenditure on youth is deemed to be not welfare but an "investment in the future of society", writes Dr Merke[1], the German Federal Minister for Women and Youth, in her foreword to the KJHG (6th Edition 1994).

The changes in the legislation reflect the debates on the relative positions of parents, children and the state and greater recognition of the importance of the family and the state as partners.

In Germany the traditional concept of 'parental powers' was changed in the wording of the constitution to 'parental care' in 1980, binding the state and its agents to support and monitor the vigilance of parents in the fulfilment of their duty to care for and educate their children. In England and Scotland child care legislation changed the concept of 'parental rights' into 'parental responsibility' with the explicit directive for continuing parental responsibility even after the removal of their legal powers, indicating thereby the importance of the continuation of parental involvement. (Children Act 1989, England and Wales, Children (Scotland) Act 1995).

Whilst the Children Acts in England and Scotland target a specific group of 'children in need' the KJHG in Germany specifies the kinds of help that are available and leaves it to the discretion of judges, social workers and parents to decide which are most appropriate in each case without a definition of need as such. One of the universal provisions introduced, for instance, is nursery education for all children over three which was to be introduced over a period of five years. In the Flemish part of Belgium the Youth Assistance Act 1990 replaces the former Youth Protection Act (1965) and distinguishes between voluntary and judicial aid. It may be too early to chart the changes which will arise from these legislative and administrative initiatives on a European level but we know from recent enquiries into the workings of the Children Act 1989 in England how new policies have changed social work practice in child and family care (Dartington Social Research Unit 1995). We also know that the theoretical framework of social work practice has changed and that a much more task focused approach has gained recognition, often in the context of discussions on how clients or users could be 'empowered', could be engaged in 'contracts', or could be seen as 'service users' rather than 'clients' in an increasingly market-oriented climate of social care and service. Working with families, which social workers had always done, became a discipline in its own right through the influence of systems theory and the recognition in the psychiatric field that relational and ecological contexts were important factors in the evolution of mental illness. Some of the flavour of these changes in the direction of 'shared responsibility', 'child-centredness' and 'task-centredness' was also detectable in the conversations with our colleagues abroad. They were more attuned to using systemic frameworks to inform their thinking about the family and used hypotheses to explore different strategies for their intervention. Since they were less hindered by the need to follow procedures they could explore how to proceed with greater degrees of freedom and diversity between professionals from different agencies. Instead of a checklist of do's and don'ts most practitioners on the continent seemed to operate from basic social work and child care principles like how to approach the family, how to obtain trust, how to assess harm and need, and how to enlist the help of other agencies.

In this brief overview we aim to compare the views and comments of those practitioners who participated in the study and reach conclusions about how their respective practices reflect ideas and thinking about the current social work task in relation to:

- working in 'partnership' with parents, young people and the community within the legal, social and cultural context of each country;
- working with risk in relation to children and young people, again in the context of the different systems;
- working with cultural difference.

## Working in partnership

The concept of 'partnership' was, until recently, not associated with social work or child care at all but tended to be used in business and in the context of professional partnerships bound by contracts and agreements which mediate differentials in power relationships, varying positions and expertise and draw boundaries around legitimate and illegitimate actions. Partnerships are about working relationships towards a common aim and are, tradition-ally at least, defined by partnership rules. The word 'partnership' does not imply equality but common purpose and the setting-up of goals for achieving the aim or purpose. Purpose and goals are usually defined before a contract for partnership is drawn up. It may be important to add here that not all fruitful partnerships are bound by contracts but usually have a purpose.

Talking about working in partnership with parents appeared to be a familiar concept to the social workers who participated in the study. Although no definition was given it did seem to mean working in 'collaboration' with parents and children and wider community systems. How this was to be achieved varied in each system and the precise meaning of the word altered with each context because of the cultural and historical differences. (See Chapter 6). In England, for instance, practitioners pondered on how one worked "in partnership with the rights of parents" and, at the same time, saw their children without their knowledge or agreement. This was no problem in those countries where the counselling of children without parental agreement was seen as legitimate and in their interest (e.g. Germany, Belgium, the Netherlands) and as part of the overall strategy of engaging with the whole family eventually.

To our colleagues in the former East German province of Mecklenburg and Vorpommern the word 'partnership' was not familiar at all, but they liked the idea very much and saw it as collaboration between the social work agency (statutory or voluntary) and families. They described a clear difference in their role and relationship to clients under the former communist system, which they thought had offered a safer community based 'net' for children at risk and the new, in their view less protective social structures of the West, which left children and young people more at risk but had given them, as professionals the opportunity to approach families with an offer of 'a package of services' under the new Act. Under the communist system, the 'community', which consisted of workplace, school, kindergarten and neigh-bourhood, had 'collaborated' to protect children. The official youth office was only called in if all else failed, thereby acquiring an interventionist and punitive role. Following the re-unification of the two Germanys in 1989, which was seen as both positive and negative from their perspective, people were less 'communally bound', more individual and separate. With the introduction of preventive measures, like the social pedagogues who work intensively with families, or the local crisis intervention centres which work with teenagers, "most families are receptive and say, yes we will accept this help, so that it is possible for the children to remain at home". The social workers in both German prac- titioners groups recognised the pitfalls inherent in the offer of provisions which have to be paid out of the community's funds and are subject to fiscal censorship when money is not available. But they saw this not so much as their problem but as the state's problem or the community's, which would have to be tackled jointly with the family as citizens. Partnership seemed to be about building an alliance for a common purpose or a relationship with the explicit aim of identifying shared concerns.

In all discussions about the hypothetical case, be they in Britain, Scotland, or on the continent, there seemed to be an assumption or even belief that this common purpose could be established, but the ways of going about it were different. They varied from approaching the mother from a feminist perspective with offers of help, to approaching the children via school and nursery and repeated attempts at gaining access to the family in order to gain a better understanding of the difficulties. In most discussions on the continent and in England and Scotland the aim of offering help and services was linked to the belief that these would be accepted and that an entrance into the family system could thereby be achieved. The most single striking difference did not lie in the social workers' analysis or preliminary assessment of the situation but in the structures which dictated their actions and which, for English social workers meant a concentration on child protection procedures from the very beginning. (See Chapter 4).

In their book entitled *Good Intentions: Developing Partnership in Social Services*, Marsh and Fisher present the results of their collaborative collective research on the topic and state that:

"Partnership practice may be defined as collaborative work towards common goals designed to solve, or reduce social problems. These goals may be agreed with the user because they are the user's wish to work on or they may be agreed with the client as a result of some external authority placing them on the client's agenda via legal proceedings. The mandate from users will be based on *their* views, while the mandate from the legal proceedings will be based on the *courts'* views." (Marsh & Fisher, 1992, p.18).

This division of mandates appeared to present fewer difficulties in other countries than in England. In Scotland, for instance, social workers referred to themselves as 'agents of the state' at the point where they had to become involved. But since they have to refer the case for further action and investigation to the children's panel and to the reporter they are free to concentrate on engaging with the family or the children, rather like their colleagues on the continent. In the English group discussion it emerged that the dilemma of having to work with these two mandates seemed to be bedevilled by the social worker's position in the courts as party to adversarial proceedings and due process. The gathering of evidence necessary for legal interventions seemed to sap energy and appeared to make the task of working out a partnership relationship more difficult although this was by no means a unanimous view. The colleagues from abroad were often puzzled by the function of these proceedings and the need to provide evidence. "You make a sort of policeman of the social worker". They were, however, also curious about the role of the guardian ad litem and the recourse to in-house legal advice. "We could do with our own lawyers, since we cannot always rely on the judge to give us the advice we need", was one comment from Germany. A judge in the German family court hinted at conflict in roles similar to England when she commented that "social workers are there to assist us in the investigation, but they often refuse as they think this spoils their relationship with the family." (Judge in the Family Court in Hamburg, 1995). This is a familiar point of view for English social workers who have no such choice.

Practitioners in all group discussions struggled with the task of wanting to engage the parents with the aim to protect the children although the partnership as such was not used. "How can we approach this family in a non-threatening way?" asked one of the workers from Belgium, "the more we intervene the more they withdraw". The need to engage parents, to gain their co-operation and goodwill was seen as the primary aim by the majority although there were differences in the way people wanted to achieve this goal. The colleague quoted above, for instance, was vigorously opposed in his aim of engaging the parents and involving them in a participatory role by his female colleague from a different agency. She stated that for her "their viewpoints are not very important in the first instance... it will take years before you can openly discuss incest... I think you should take the children as your starting point and not the situation of the parents". Both viewpoints were represented in other discussions. "We must first have a better idea of whether this mother is able to protect her children... talking to them would for me be the first step" was the suggestion of a worker in one of the German groups. "We can do a lot of damage by tearing in there, undermining responsibility... whereas we could harness it, engaging it and actually giving it back to the parents, which is appropriate", was a consensus view in several English discussions. Unfortunately the way to achieve this goal seemed to be paved with procedural obstacles and disagreement about whether to call a planning meeting, a strategy meeting or no meeting at all at stage one or two.

Working through the children without parental knowledge was not acceptable in England, France or Italy but featured prominently in discussions in the Flemish system, in Holland and in Germany. Here workers in the specialist child protection service (*Kinderschutzdienst* or KSD) spoke of an "internal, straight line" of professional confidence which guided actions or non-actions. "We can afford to work in the pre-field of intervention, ... we can use time to build up relationships". This included relationships within the professional network, models of co-working and offers of family and individual work. The overall aim would always be to engage with the whole family and to co-opt members of the extended family, like the grandmother, if necessary. There certainly would have been a helpers' conference (*Helferkonferenz*) at stage two or even earlier, depending on agency policy, which is a kind of strategy meeting. The youth office would have called such a meeting for advice and a general pooling of ideas which might include the offer of temporary accommodation for the daughter if she agreed, not only for protection but also to introduce change into a family system which is stuck. If nothing worked and as a last resort the appropriate legal authority could be called in to exert additional power and pressure, as children can be accommodated without parental permission on a 24 hour basis at the request of a social worker and with little more than a telephone call or a fax giving brief details. Both German teams worked similarly, using the recent legislation to its full advantage and aiming at collaboration with at least one parent.

Another perception of how a partnership-like relationship along the model suggested by Marsh and Fisher (1992) might be established was suggested by an Italian colleague who proposed that the courts needed to be involved as arbitrators or mediators 'to break the deadlock', within the system, since "a resort to the authority of the judge enables us to find ways of re-establishing a relationship with the family so that help can be offered". The courts were seen strategically, as hierarchically superior institutions, which were able to mediate between or dictate action to parties who were caught in a dispute about private rights and public responsibilities, not equal in power but maybe equal in their state of 'deadlock'.

French social workers, in their discussion of the hypothetical case, debated at which point to refer to the children's judge and how to work with the play centre where Andrew, the second child in the story, is placed. In France the children's judge can be involved at an earlier stage and could have been approached by the grandmother directly. As in other countries the French clearly recognised the importance of giving parents the chance of working towards a better situation for the children before making decisions about them. "As soon as someone has children, he has the duty to educate them...and we have the duty to aid them". This spirit of collaboration in France appears to be informed by a consensus view on how the state and the family can work together even when they disagree.

In the former East Germany all practitioners were members of the district youth office team and had long experience of working in the previous communist system which they could now evaluate with the benefit of hindsight and the knowledge of another way of doing things. They were more confident than most of being able to establish at least a working relationship by patiently chiselling away and approaching the family from all angles before involving the court, "it is part of our cultural background to look for solutions in the community", they said. One practitioner identified the locus of the dilemma inherent in her role: "If I want to protect these children I have to go and go again, I must work on these parents to get them to see *my problem*." This echoes to some extent what Marsh and Fisher (1992) say: "In the case of an external mandate deriving from legal process there may well be some degree of 'persuading' the client that a problem seen by others has to be a problem for them." (ibid p.18).

In all countries the idea of working in partnership was not restricted to families but included other agencies, like schools, the nursery, specialists such as therapists, psychologists, the family doctor. Planning meetings for goal setting which involve older children and members of the family seemed to take place in all countries but there is not sufficient information in the data gathered to make direct comparisons with the kind of meetings that form part of the procedures in England. The social workers seemed to work more within their respective agencies using their professional authority to involve others, including courts, as

necessary. The English system of networking, which was demonstrated in the video taped discussions, was admired and appreciated, especially in those countries where the representatives
from different services found how little they knew about each
other's structures and ways of working whilst they were addressing
the hypothetical case material.

The involvement of the police as partners in child protection
procedures in England is unique and was not understood at all well
by colleagues on the continent even after detailed explanations. It
shows how much work has gone into the joint child protection
team work here in England that the researchers had such difficulty
in being able to understand the objections to joint child protection
procedures fully. The police on the continent are involved in child
protection, however, and can deal with cases without reference to
statutory agencies. Like everyone else they can refer children and
parents to specialist services if necessary and apply to the courts
for emergency protection.

In several countries, notably Germany, Belgium and the
Netherlands with their confidential doctor systems, partnership
practice also involves the older children or those who can clearly
state their view and preferences. Lack of procedural pressures
frees up time to engage, create trust and explore choices as
described above. In England and Scotland older children are also
involved in decisions concerning their future and are consulted,
but unless they are in care, this usually happens only with the
agreement of parents.

The 'landscape of provisions', referred to by the colleague in the
former East German province, was in most countries provided by
a mixture of voluntary and statutory organisations. One of the
most valued services in Germany seemed to be the skilled 'social
pedagogues' or specialist social workers, who can be attached to
highly disorganised or needy families for periods up to two years as
part of an intensive programme to help a family 'help itself' in the
management of the task of educating its children. Pedagogy or
education here does not only refer to schools but is used in the
broad sense of a family's ability to develop and teach children the
skills they need to get on in life, to acquire confidence and a sense
of responsibility. These specialists are social workers or social
pedagogues with additional training in working closely with
families through periods of engagement, consolidation and dis-
engagement. The advantage of such intensive family based
intervention, which is not subject to court orders but can be
reviewed by the court, is recognised by writing the provision of this
service into the KJHG (1990). Like other services and provisions it
can be used as the basis for negotiation either to keep children at

home or to return them if they have been in voluntary or statutory care. Accommodation in foster families or children's homes and residential treatment centres for short periods appears to be more acceptable in Germany and France (we have little data about the other countries), especially when this is worked out as part of an overall plan with parents or a parent. Apart from adoption all orders are revocable and all interventions, so it seems, are directed at keeping a child in its family unless there really is no other alternative.

In countries other than Britain, there was no equivalent of the child protection conference, nor an equivalent of administrative power being shared by a multidisciplinary body of people who meet and deliberate whether a child needs to be registered for protection or not. The Flemish mediation committee and the informal hearing in the judge's rooms, which take place in Germany and France, appeared to be better suited for collaborative practice or practice where authoritative power has to be demonstrated without the recourse to legal intervention yet with a clear mandate that it could have recourse to legal intervention if necessary. Their coercive function is explicit and stated in a context where negotiation is possible and where choices can be made.

Marsh and Fisher refer in this context to the "third mandate of the case conference" in England in connection with child protection registration, where the directives given by the case conference have no legal status, yet are powerful in that they carry consequences. (Marsh and Fisher, p.22-23). They constitute a form of compulsory intervention without legal safeguards. This can be confusing for parents and social workers and was confusing for our colleagues abroad. "Whom is it for, this conference with all these people?" was one of the questions, "it might be a good idea for keeping us (professionals) to our task but how do the family feel, sitting together with so many strange people?"

An English social worker commented in one of the discussion groups on seeing other systems at work: "There is a very dishonest overall notion that everybody is somehow equally responsible and equally involved...in reality it doesn't work".

England is the only country with elaborate child protection procedures where professionals have to report abuse to the police or the social services department, and where there is a register of children at risk. Other countries have administrative ways of negotiating with parents and children according to their respective guidelines and traditions but they do not seem to have to work with a 'third mandate' since there is no registration. English social workers in the discussion groups commented repeatedly on how colleagues in other countries appeared to have less difficulty in applying partnership practice in the context of child protection because their tasks seemed clearer. Some thought that the lack of procedures could result in children being less well protected and were puzzled by the variety of different approaches. One social worker stated wistfully:

> "The power not to act: not to be involved in the legal process. Child protection procedures are streamlined the moment there is an allegation. It feels that the whole statutory thing takes over. I feel that's a loss in our system". (Hetherington *et al.*, 1996 p.44).

Another commented:

> "The inquisitorial nature of the legal system minimised the conflict between families and social workers and enabled more co-operative approach to problem solving." (*ibid.*, p.50)

Colleagues on the continent noticed how similar the discussion on the dilemma of the social work task was in England when faced with non-co-operation and clear signs of risk to both children. Yet they seemed less powerless and stuck in the face of non-co-operation, they could act with authority and confidence in more diverse systems. The responsibility for interventions could be shared with the court, the special judge, the mediation service, the confidential doctor, the reporter or the office of the prosecutor.

"The risks we have to take are greater, but we are not held as directly responsible when a child is harmed as you seem to be in England" was one observation from abroad. Does this lead to more risks for children in those countries with whom we compared social work practice? The following case illustrates how risk can be handled differently without conclusions on what may be better or worse since different ways of addressing the same problem is, as we have seen, not really a professional matter but a matter of systems, cultures, and historical developments.

## Working with risk: a story from Germany

The following story was told by a mother in the province of Rheinland Pfalz, Germany. Her history forms part of another research project which compares parents' stories of their experiences with child care systems in England, France (Baistow *et al.*, 1996) and Germany (research in progress). Also recorded are the comments by English social workers on what would have

happened to this family in England. Below is an abridged version
of both sets of interviews.

## The first part of the story

Mrs S had moved from one of the former communist countries in
the East to West Germany as part of the repatriation policy which
followed the collapse of the communist system. She was a single
parent and brought with her two children, a son of ten and a girl of
eight. Her son could not settle in the new town nor in the school
and played her up to the point where she felt out of control. He
stole from shops although he was never reported. She always
found out because she was told privately. Eventually she told his
teacher at school that she had reached a point of such despair and
rage that she 'beat him black and blue', hoping the teacher might
suggest something that helped. The teacher, however, did not.
Later the mother found out that the teacher tried to protect her
son by not telling the mother when he misbehaved. Mrs S did not
want to contact the youth office as she only knew them as statutory
services who took children away. But in the end she had no choice
and found that, contrary to her expectations, they referred her and
her son to an after school centre to which her son was taken from
school, where he could stay, do his homework, get some
counselling and where she and her daughter were also invited to
group sessions with other families. He was brought home at 6pm.
   The comments by English social workers at this point were
directed at what they perceived as 'negligence' by the school
teacher in not intervening when the mother approached her. They
enquired about relevant policies and procedures and were told
that there were guidelines which stipulated that the teacher should
initially have tried to help or advise Mrs S as to what she could do
or what services she could approach. If this did not work she could
and indeed should have either referred the mother to the youth
office or referred her to the school psychological service, or the
educational guidance service. She could have informed her head of
year or school and asked for further guidance about how to help.
But there was no obligation, only a recommendation that she
should act in this way.
   In England Mrs S's approach to the teacher would have led to an
investigation, including a medical examination and, depending on
the severity of the beating, probably to a child protection
conference. Her son might have been put on the child protection
register. An assessment of need would have been made and
depending on its outcome several things might have happened. As

the mother wanted help she and the children could have been referred to the local child guidance or family centre where he might have been offered individual counselling and the mother parent group work. The whole family could have been involved in family therapy. He could have been accommodated for respite care if Mrs S wanted this. The emphasis in the British system would have been on getting the mother to take her son to appropriate services; depending on the assessment of need there might have been an allocated social worker, who would review progress regularly.

This was, in fact, what happened in Germany once Mrs S had contacted the youth office without, however, the statutory involvement of the case conference or the involvement of other professional disciplines. Mrs S thought that she and the social worker made the decisions.

*The second part of the story*

Going to the centre helped initially and the family attended for over 16 months. Although Mrs S found it useful, the relationship between her and her son did not improve that much; he still defied her, associated with older skin heads, continued stealing and painted swastikas over the school and ran away for a whole weekend after having been confronted at the centre for his behaviour. He refused to return to it. He was accused of arson and the police appeared in uniform at Mrs S's door. Her son was 12 by now. Mrs S contacted the social worker again and begged her to take her son away as she felt close to a nervous breakdown. He did not want to go. The staff at the centre, who were consulted, also thought he should remain with her and that they could help her manage him better. After another very bad fight, when Mrs S again beat her son, he phoned the social worker himself and asked to be taken away. She responded immediately and took him to a foster family who lived in the same town. The boy refused to stay there. He was moved to a group home where he was happier but still exposed to local influences and older boys. Mrs S and the social worker debated the risks of this. Both agreed that the social worker would try to work with her son individually. She made herself available to him to visit her in her office which he did when he felt like it. Eventually he agreed to go and see a group home away from the town and a special school 'just to see what it was like'. He then decided to stay. Mrs S thought that this involvement of her son in the decision about him had helped and that her son would not have co-operated otherwise. She was, against all expectations, glad about the help her son was receiving and glad too that she was to be included in the on-going work with him and the family while he was at the group home and attending a special school for children with behavioural difficulties.

The comments of the English colleagues reflected their surprise that the social worker could and did respond so quickly to the boy's request rather than the mother's at the earlier stage, thereby leaving the boy in an emotionally and physically abusive situation. They also wondered about the daughter and the apparent absence of a risk assessment involving the whole family. They were also surprised that the social worker could act with such apparent authority, introducing the boy to different facilities which, in the English system, would come under different administrative structures. A special school placement could not be set up without involving the education authority, would entail statementing procedures and certainly debates over which authority was responsible for funding the special school

*The end of the story*

At this point of the interview Mrs S had visited her son twice and he had been home for the Easter break. Both made efforts to remain calm. His sister had been glad to see him as she missed him. Mrs S feels hopeful that their relationship would improve and was pleased that she had been closely involved in all discussions between the social worker and the new school and in the formulation of a help plan for her son. She thought that her son would not have co-operated had she insisted on him going away, he would have run off and would have been at a greater risk of getting into bad company.

The English social workers commented that the difference in the social work approach to the problem was, in the end, not as great as it first seemed and that the outcome might have been the same in both countries. The different organisational structures, however, had left the German social worker free to work in a child-centred way, gaining his co-operation gradually whilst keeping his mother informed and involved. As case worker for the patch in which the family lived she remained the key contact for the family and held the co-ordinating role between the family and other services for two years and more.

Research in England confirms the importance of continuity in social workers, especially when they are involved with families suffering abuse where relationships are slow to grow, but found that this was only happening in a few cases. When parents were fully

involved in the child protection conference and felt engaged in the
process the outcome was more likely to be positive for children
than when this is not happening. (Thoburn, J. *et al.*, 1995)

In their discussion of this case the English social workers
thought that it would probably have been most likely that this
family would have been referred on after an initial duty assessment
as the mother appeared to be resourceful and co-operative. It
depended on what resources were available. But at the later stage,
when things deteriorated, the case might have been re-referred to
them and the youth justice team might have become involved. The
procedural framework in England would certainly have led to an
earlier intervention and might have prevented further escalation,
but this was not certain and depended on thresholds of need,
availability of and access to resources. They thought that in this
case the risk of further abuse would have been smaller because of
the requirement to intervene at the point of the initial contact with
the teacher which would have brought in protection procedures.
Procedures are therefore in the first instance, designed to ensure
good practice and in the second to review progress and outcome
but at what cost?

This question preoccupied the social workers who commented
on the above case. They thought that Mrs S had retained her role
as mother in charge throughout and this had been important to
her. The patch system ensured continuity which is often disrupted
in England through the duty system and the categorisation of cases
into short and long-term work. They were surprised at the
apparent absence of 'assessments' or signs of delays in order to
obtain assessments. They would not have liked to have carried the
risk of leaving the boy in an abusive situation but agreed that it
would have been difficult to keep him away from home against his
wishes.

The English social workers commented repeatedly on the
"freedom to act and the freedom from responsibility to investigate" which they observed on video in the discussions by their
colleagues abroad and again in this case. It appeared to enable a
more "co-operative approach to problem solving". They found
that there appeared to be more "user-friendly legal systems" in
other countries and that there was more support for social workers
to take risks and work in a more creative and flexible way.
Throughout the discussions of several English groups who commented on systems in other European countries there seemed to
be a degree of envy for their colleagues who worked within a
framework of law and procedure that gave them a great deal more
freedom to work in partnership with families and achieve change.

## Working with cultural difference

The case history above gives some indication of how differences in the experience of services and institutions affect the expectation and choice of a parent seeking help. The English social workers were quick to highlight the fact that Mrs S had come from a different political system which must have affected her expectation of services and her perspective on the society in which she now lived. This did not seem to have played a noticeable part in the German social workers' handling of the case although we only have Mrs S's story. It was interesting, however, how this question of cultural difference in the background of the family and the effect of migration on the children, especially the older boy was picked up by the team in England.

It confirmed the impression gained in the previous study and earlier comparative work (Cooper et al., 1995) that race and culture differences are viewed differently on the continent and that different assumptions and values apply.

In the course of the structured research discussions on the hypothetical case one question focused on cultural difference. Would the social workers have acted differently, had the family been black? As researchers we soon realised that this question, which had been designed with British social workers in mind, was inappropriate in the context of other European countries where it had to be adapted to take account of different experiences. Whereas the English social workers in their discussions of the hypothetical case were keenly aware of the importance of antidiscriminatory practice, it seemed that social workers on the continent would approach the same question with ideas about different cultural values but no apparent reference to their role in antidiscriminatory practice.

Immigrants in France, for instance, are expected to conform to notions of French 'citizenship and an integrationist mentality'. (Cooper et al., 1995, p.133). In Italy the notion that 'when in Rome do as the Romans do' was not exactly stated but implied by the remark that "People from outside the EC would need help to understand our laws". The participants were mostly unequivocal in their view that their aim of protecting the children would not be affected by cultural differences but that their thinking about how to proceed might be: "we have cultural intermediaries who understand their way of looking at things and their traditions".

In France the ideology of integration is central in questions relating to race and culture. Immigrants and minorities are respected for their difference but are also expected to conform to the norms of the French Republic while living there. "Talking about a North African family, we can respect their way of living and their culture but within the limits of violence and danger for children...it is true that parents can be considered with our vision as violent but not violent through the eyes of their children...but it is true that there is a threshold of tolerance, a level defined by us, based on the standards of common life", said one worker in the French discussion group. In the Walloon part of Belgium a similar, but more differentiated view was expressed: "I think one has to approach it differently, one has to look at it not from the point of view of our laws but of theirs. But all the same, they are in our country, and that is where the confrontation lies". In one of the English discussions someone spoke about the "implicit fear about being perceived as being racist when you go there to investigate a child protection situation, so it's a sense of being disempowered which is why it is very important to hold onto the fact that your primary focus is child protection and those are the issues that matter". None of the colleagues on the continent expressed this nor did they refer to their own institutionalised racism or differences in the power relationships as a result of racial difference. These ideas did not seem to be readily available in the context of talking about child protection.

In the English groups, on the other hand, the question on racial difference and anti-discriminatory practice sparked off a lively debate which was considerably more confident and wider ranging than the earlier discussion on child protection procedures and checklists. Colleagues abroad noticed and commented on the level of awareness in the debate of this question and of needing to learn how to practice in an antidiscriminatory way. They reflected on the learning process in England which still had to take place in their own country.

In both parts of Germany the question was greeted with interest. The colleagues in Rostock, where not so long ago a house for immigrants had been burnt down, were sensitive to racial discrimination and the threat of racially fuelled violence in a structurally insecure environment. There had been a huge influx of people from the East who were culturally different and were often discriminated against on the basis of their difference because of the threat they posed to the local job market. They considered integration and equal opportunity as a primary aim and hoped that this could be achieved in a few years. On racial discrimination they wanted guidance because there were few black people in their region. One social worker had been on study leave to America and had encountered considerable racial discrimination there against black and Hispanic people. She feared that it might be 'imported' from the West as part of the process of becoming a capitalist economy.

In Rheinland Pfalz, the group debated at length how they might proceed, if the family had come from Turkey, or the East of Europe, as so many do who live in their region. Similar points were made, they also had a 'specialist' who worked mainly with Turkish families. They mentioned that there were few black people in their area and therefore little experience of working with them in professional contexts.

It became clear that the question about racial difference did have a different meaning in each country and that the debate, which was happening in England, did not seem to be going on here or, if it was, we did not hear of it. There were different perceptions of racial discrimination and, unlike in child protection, it did not seem to be a debate about shared values and professional practice in different systems. A different question might have highlighted the complexities better and would have given us more information about the social, political and legal structures into which the meaning of cultural and racial differences were embedded in each country.

## Reflections

What do we see when we look at reflections of our practice through the eyes of those in other countries?

"The child protection social work role in foreign systems appears to be easier than in England. Ease of access to the legal sphere, relative legal informality and flexibility, separation between investigation and intervention, and a relative absence of conflicts of individual rights in favour of prioritising children's needs appeared to be the principal factors which combine to produce this overall response." (Hetherington *et al.*, 1996, p.100).

These were the main factors which repeatedly occurred in discussions together with a certain anxiety about the apparent lack of checks and procedures in other systems to ensure that children were, in fact, protected. Other concerns centred on the apparent lack of focus on parental versus children's rights.

Social workers who remembered their work years ago, before 'Beckford' and subsequent public enquiries, were reminded of how they too were once able to be more flexible, less bound by procedural rules and by what one team leader called the "whole industry around child protection". At the same time, however, they expressed fear of returning to a system which was less vigorous, more 'dangerously relaxed", as if there was only a choice between one or the other. The evidence of this comparative research has shown that most of the systems under scrutiny abroad and in Scotland stressed family support and diversity in services along the lines of the main conclusions in Messages from Research. (Dartington Social Research Unit, 1995).

What appeared to be missing in the English debate but was implicit in most of the discussions in other countries was a sense of professional confidence and trust which social workers abroad seem to have in finding a way forward. This was especially noticeable in countries with a strong religious tradition of family values and a national constitution where the joint responsibility of state and parents to children is spelt out in the constitution and forms the basis of the legal and administrative systems which are relevant to them. The social workers in all countries other than England felt less 'attacked' and better supported in their task by the administrative and legal systems of their country. There was not the same sense of having to battle on two fronts like their colleagues in England whose discussion had been permeated by references to procedures which provided guidelines but also interfered with professional judgement.

All the child protection systems we studied make clear provision for responding to both children's needs and their protection, and make available coercive powers so that this response can be enforced where family co-operation is absent. The foreign systems described in the research appeared to enable social workers to achieve a working balance between welfare and protection which seemed close to one of the statements made by the Department of Health in the report quoted above:

> "An approach that encourages a perspective on cases as children in need in circumstances where there may be a protection problem is more likely to lead to a wider range of services being used to ensure the child's safety and recovery". (Dartington Social Research Unit, 1995, p.48).

The English system by contrast and on the evidence gathered, appears to function in terms of "children who need protection and who also have needs". (Hetherington 1996 *et al.*, p.101). This does create a difference for social workers who need and want to intervene yet often cannot do so because of the adversarial nature of the legal system and the need to comply with procedures. There is no room for the kind of negotiation referred to above or the wider considerations that could lead to alternative avenues. Social workers in the English system reported that they often find themselves trapped in a situation where they would like to engage and work with families but must attend to their legal and procedural duties.

The social work task itself, however, the thinking about priorities and goals and the use of systemic frameworks was very similar in all countries despite the differences in administrative structures, cultures and legal systems. This confirms the existence of a professional culture and identity which, despite the differences, is able to speak a common language. The enjoyment and enthusiasm of the participants is proof of interest in and curiosity about different ways of working and using this difference as a tool to reflect on one's own practice. The experience was summed up fittingly by the team leader in the district of Bad Doberan, in Rostock: "We really enjoyed this exercise, it made us think and it took us out of our groove. We only wish we had more time as we touched on so many important things in these brief discussions. We believe that we could learn a lot from each other."

# Chapter 9:
# The child, the family, the state and the social worker

The phrase 'child protection' is understood differently in different parts of Europe. In general it is given a wider meaning in continental Europe, and would frequently be understood to refer to matters such as employment legislation protecting children against exploitation, and the protection of children outside the family rather more than within the family. We have not found elsewhere a phrase that equates to 'child protection' meaning intra-familial protection, as it is used in the UK. In this chapter, we are looking at intra-familial child protection; not the relationship between children and society, as in the wider meaning of the phrase, but at the relationship demonstrated in our case scenario between the child, its family and the state. It is indeed interesting that the UK differs from the rest of Europe in its identification of what children need to be protected *from*; but this is another issue, and not directly addressed by our research.

## The state and the family

The development of the relationship between the state and families is fundamental to modern society. Lorraine Fox Harding writes:

> "Consideration of the workings of child care laws and machinery of the state, and the ideas underlying them, may contribute to an understanding of the role of the state in general." (Fox Harding, 1991 p.5).

Donzelot describes the development of this relationship and the role of the state in France (Donzelot 1980) in terms of the emergence of the social sphere. His description makes it clear that the modern relationship between the state and the family will have been influenced by a wide range of possible factors including history, religion, culture and socio-economic factors, and is therefore certain to have emerged differently in all countries. Nevertheless, common to all the countries we studied, is the emergence of the interest of the state in the well-being of children as future citizens. This is shown in a range of ways, including legislation of the kind described by other countries as 'child protection'. The range also includes legislation and services for direct protective intervention by the state between parent and child. A description of a country's child protection system and the way it is operated describes the nature of the bargain between the state and parents over the upbringing of children, a process in which both parents and state have interests that may conflict. It also describes the position of children as independent, or not so independent, individuals. In the process of describing their child protection systems and the ways in which they would expect them to operate, the social workers gave us their view of the expectations that parents and the state have of their relationship with each other in the task of bringing up children, and where the social work profession fits into this.

Although the labels may be different, all the countries we studied, (and as far as we know, all countries in the European Union), have legislation and administrative practice that regulate the points at which the state should intervene in the family between parent and child. This goes beyond the provision of universal services such as health and education which may at different times or in various circumstances be compulsory or non-compulsory, or of targeted benefits such as financial allowances. What we are concerned with is the point at which, and the manner in which, the state is prepared to overrule the rights of parents; the rights to look after their children and to make their own decisions, within the laws of the land, as to what is best for their children. This is the crunch point in the relationship between parents and the state, and demonstrates the contract between the state and its citizens and future citizens.

## The state and social workers

In all the countries we studied social work was, in varying degrees, seen as representing the state. This was felt less strongly by workers in some voluntary organisations, but for all, there was some part of the social work profession, (represented in the research group and accepted as a working colleague), which had a clear role as an intermediary between what the state required or offered, and the family. However, as has been described in Chapter 6, this role varied between different countries, and different aspects of it were differently distributed. The relationship of the social worker to the state is demonstrated by what happens when social workers are in conflict with parents. The expectations of the social workers of their own behaviour gives a picture not only of their relationship to the family and parents, but also of their relationship to the state.

There are many different ways of distributing the task of state intervention, and the expectations of social workers about their own role are affected by the relationships between the state and the law, and the state and the police. During the development of the case scenario, we can see demonstrated various models of how the social work role can be defined. At some stage, all models reached a point at which the social worker had to consider using the power of the state to intervene in the family between parents and children. There was, however, considerable variation between the countries as to the degree of dilemma that this posed for the social worker and the point at which the dilemma arose. There was considerable variation in the confidence which social workers demonstrated in their relationship with the state.

An important factor in the relationship between state and social worker derives from the nature of the legal system. An adversarial legal system sets up a triangular system where the law is arbiter between the state and the parent. In the inquisitorial legal system, the law is proactive. There are differences between all the continental systems for child law that we studied, but they were all inquisitorial rather than adversarial systems, and all their systems allowed for the active intervention of the judge for children as protector rather than as arbiter.

Differences between the systems were tabulated in Chapter 3. What follows is a more detailed examination of the responses of the groups of social workers to the case scenario in relation to their power as agents of the state. It should be noted that for several of the continental systems, referral to the judge for children was channelled through the office of the public procurator, who had the power to take emergency action and to initiate emergency police investigations. The procurator could refuse to make a referral to the judge, but the social workers did not refer to this as a factor to be taken into consideration. This system locates police action and formal investigation squarely in the judicial sphere.

## France

The judge for children in France has been described as taking on the roles carried by police and social workers in Britain (Garrapon 1993); the judge controls and sets up the investigation and the framework of intervention. The French system encourages the early intervention of the judge for children in a way not replicated in the other systems we studied. In the first stage of the case scenario, the French social workers made the assumption that if there was a likelihood of risk, danger or developmental difficulties because of family problems, there was a duty for the social workers to respond; one possible response would be referral to the judge for children. It was not expected, but would be possible. There was no sign of tension between the social workers' concerns and their capacity to act. By the second stage, where Andrew is referred for the first time, the social workers were more actively considering involving the judge. They would have preferred to use voluntary approaches, but their purpose was to reach the children in the context of the family, and compulsion was a possibility. This attitude continued in the third stage. The fundamental project was to address the children's needs, the judge could enable this and should be used to do this if necessary.

By the last stage, there was agreement that a referral should by now have been made to the judge. There was no uncertainty about the appropriateness of judicial action or their capacity to activate this. Where parents are failing to protect their children, or fulfil the essential conditions of their upbringing, then it is the state's duty to intervene and ensure that the matter is addressed. Although there was little hesitation about using compulsion where necessary, workers did not ignore the impact that this could or would have on relationships with the family, and they were aware that trust and co-operation might be compromised. But though they deliberated and pondered different strategies, they did so with the confidence that they could pursue the judicial route should they so wish.

## Italy

In Italy the first stage of the scenario did not provoke much anxiety in the social workers. The social workers wondered why there should be any expectation that they as social workers should be involved if the family were not asking for help. Referral to the judge was mentioned as a theoretical possibility in a worst case situation, but as not applicable at this point. The social workers saw themselves as offering the possibility of help, if that help was actively sought by the family. They were clear that they did not consider that they had any professional duty to inquire into the situation. At the second stage, some of the workers were thinking about informal consultation with the judge. The state, as represented by the judiciary, was seen as an external authority, available to be called on by the social workers, but not central to their professional task. The social workers were emphatic that they were not investigators, but agents for bringing about change in the family. They considered that they had no right to intervene in the family unless the family wished; they wanted to work with the family, and might be able to make use of the authority of the judiciary to enable that. By the third stage, the social workers were increasingly inclined to involve the judge, now not just for consultation, but for action. The social workers were using the judge as a source of authority which they lacked in their own role. They did not refer the family on the basis of investigations, but as a way of making a statement about the seriousness of the situation that might enable the social workers to engage the parents.

By the last stage, there was no hesitation about referral to the judge. There was no mention of any need for evidence or proof; the non-co-operation of the parents provided the grounds for referral. One worker described using judicial referral as a means of 'putting a bomb under the parents', of dismantling a defensive structure which the parents were setting up around the family. This image conveyed very vividly the picture of the family as sovereign territory, and the social workers as ambassadors or negotiators from another power, only powerful in so far as power was directly and immediately delegated to them.

Although the French and Italian social workers shared a family-centred attitude in their conception of child-centred work, they demonstrated very different ways of using the judicial system. The readiness of referral in France was not replicated in Italy. The responses of the Italian social workers suggested a more distant relationship between the state and the family, and a very different attitude to parents. The parents seemed to be more powerful, and the state less interventionist; and yet the judge could play the role of a heavy father and regulate family behaviour. The Italian social workers were, of all the groups, the least impressed by the English system except for a social worker from southern Italy. She felt that in her region the judge for children always took the part of the parents, and she felt that the English system would ensure that the child was represented.

## Germany

Like the Italians, all the other groups of social workers avoided judicial intervention if possible, but in every country the framework and the nature of the dilemmas were slightly different. The German social workers were very clear about their goals and secure in their knowledge that the law enabled them to work in a particular way. This did not mean that they had no dilemmas, but it did enable them to have a constructive discussion about them. They needed to gain more information and to work confidentially, but they were well aware of the potential dangers of the situation. At the second stage, the parents' refusal to accept offers of help is seen as a trigger to call a meeting (*Helferkonferenz*) involving a wider net of professionals. As described in Chapter 8, this is not a formal procedure like a child protection conference. It is nearer to a strategy meeting, but less orientated towards immediate action. The focus is on sharing information and co-operative planning between professionals. Although the voluntary agencies (who would be as likely to be the key agency as the *Jugendamt*) would not have direct access to legal intervention at this point, they could if they felt necessary contact the *Jugendamt* who have the authority that is derived from work on judicial orders and are state employees. Legal intervention could be initiated quickly, but at the second stage they did not feel this to be necessary. At the third stage, the voluntary agency social workers would use the potential involvement of the *Jugendamt* and the courts as a lever. In their work with Frances, they would make sure that she understood that the court could protect her, and they would work with her to get her agreement to intervention with her parents by themselves, the *Jugendamt* or the court. If they thought there was serious risk to the children, a hearing with the judge could be set up at short notice, which could result in voluntary agreement or an order. Referral to the law is thus a means of entering into a further stage of negotiation with the parents, which does not necessarily lead to the use of compulsion, but may do so.

At the final stage, the social workers had to face a professional dilemma over the level of risk to Frances and the need to take time to work with her in deciding what she wanted to happen. The voluntary agency workers, who had no reporting duty in relation to child abuse, did not feel under pressure from a legal or procedural point of view, but they carried a weight of professional anxiety. How far should they leave Frances in control of what happened? When should they override her wishes because of the level of risk to both herself and her brother? When should they override her need for more time if this prevented Andrew's needs from being met? The *Jugendamt* is mandated to 'watch over' the parental duty to 'provide care, upbringing and education', so the social workers there have more of an enforcement role, but the dilemma for them was not significantly different. The difference for them lay more in other people's perception and expectation of their role. The effect of the subsidiarity principle, in increasing the importance of voluntary agency interventions, combined with the support for direct confidential work with children, seemed to give power to the professional. The reinforcement of the relationship between the child and the professional connected the child to the state. They described quite easy access to judicial power, and quite an independent position in relation to judicial power. The voluntary agency workers have the independence of their agency's status, and the *Jugendamt* workers are employees of a separate arm of the state from the judiciary, and (from other evidence than the case scenario), can disagree with the judge, who is responsible if things go wrong. The social worker is the person who judges at what point confidentiality for the child has to be overridden for the child's interests and safety. This is an enormous responsibility of which the social workers were well aware, but they seemed to feel confident and legitimated in carrying this responsibility. There was a general assumption that referral to the judge was best avoided, but the grounds were that voluntary co-operation is usually most effective, and legal referral was something that could be used strategically if helpful. In spite of the extensive use of voluntary rather than statutory agencies, the connection between the state and the social workers seemed to be very strong and the legal framework very supportive; the outsiders here were the parents.

## The Netherlands

The Netherlands shares with Germany a commitment to subsidiarity, and the extensive use of voluntary agencies in child welfare services. The structures of child protection are however considerably different. There is no equivalent to the *Jugendamt*, and the confidential doctor service was referred to as a resource throughout. At the first stage, the social workers expected to try to make contact with the family, and thought that they would be able to arrive at some level of communication with them. They held in reserve the possibility that they could contact the confidential doctor service (CDS). This service would try to make contact with the family and would preserve the anonimity of the referrer. The involvement of the CDS would signal that the situation was considered to be serious, so the social workers had a means of communicating their anxieties to the family without resorting to any official proceedings. Thus the Dutch social workers could introduce a note of official concern very easily without introducing any element of coercion. At the same time, they had a very strong commitment to making a connection with the family through their own persistence, and confidence in being able to do this. At the second stage, the social workers considered more actively the possibility of referral to the child protection board. They would only do this if they had indications that Andrew was at risk from parental violence. Referral to the CDS was still a possibility, but their expectation continued to be that they could establish a working relationship with the parents. At stage three, as in Germany, Frances had considerable power to control what happens, but the power was there for the social workers to make a decision on her behalf if they felt it to be necessary. In order to offer legal protection, an official investigation would be needed which would involve the child protection board, or be set up by the judge for children. By this point, referral to the CDS had become less relevant, and the question was whether to involve the legal system.

By the final stage, the social workers considered that compulsory measures were necessary. They would expect to make a written report to the judge and ask for an investigation. It might be that at this point the parents would begin to co-operate, and legal intervention would not be necessary, but the social workers were envisaging placement away from home for both children. The emphasis of the social workers' intervention was on the children, and questions of parental rights were not mentioned. The powers of the state were available to the social workers to use; they did not however, have to use them, and could choose not to. They did not discuss any problems about having legal grounds for state intervention. One of the social workers worked for a voluntary organisation as a guardian (see Chapter 4 — no similarity with the English guardian ad litem), but she worked closely with the judge for children. As a guardian, she was responsible for families with children on supervision orders and with children in placements. She worked with the parents and the children. This role holds considerable delegated authority as the social worker represents the judge, and works with the family to achieve the goals set by the judge. At the same time, the judge relies on the reports and assessments of the social worker to set these goals. The social worker described making strategic use of the division of the task between herself and the judge in her work with families. Another social worker who worked in an agency providing intensive short term family work for families on supervision orders, described a similar strategic use of the difference between his role and that of the guardian. The guardian was the authority figure, he was there to help the family achieve the goals set by the guardian. There seemed to be a very pragmatic acceptance of the reality of power and how it was distributed between different operators in the system, and a pragmatic use of this as a way of reaching a working relationship with the families. What stood out very strongly from the discussions of the Dutch social workers was their insistence at every stage that they would be able to get into communication with the whole family. They did not accept (although they could make hypothetical contingency plans) that it would not be possible. This was the focus of their energy, and they showed no anxiety about getting legal support if necessary. The fact that they worked for voluntary agencies did not make them any less confident in the support that they could get from the state.

Recent legislation in the Netherlands has increased the requirement for social workers to provide evidence of abuse in their reports to the judge, and has increased the emphasis on assessment. The workers were uncertain about the implications of this for practice and afraid that it would delay decisions. It was seen as an increase in parental rights, and they were anxious about the impact on children's interests. Another current change has been in the position of the CDS, which is now a part of the state system and linked to the child protection service, with a remit to monitor the prevalence of child abuse and produce statistics. The move seems to be towards a more formal and regulated system.

## Flemish Belgium

By contrast, the Belgium systems which have seen major changes do not seem to have moved towards greater formality and regulation. The focus of change there has been the deflection of families from the legal system and the promotion of negotiation. The Flemish social workers at the first stage of the case scenario were confident about working on a voluntary basis; only one worker mentioned the possibility of any problem about this, and the use of compulsion seemed a distant possibility. At the second stage there was more anxiety about the children, and one worker (based in a confidential doctor centre) was more concerned to gether information from sources outside the family, but there was generally a high level of confidence in being able to work with the situation. There were resources and alternatives available to the social workers in trying to make a positive relationship with the family. Two of these alternatives were referral to the confidential doctor centre (CDC) or to the special youth assistance service (SYA); these are still within the non-compulsory area of intervention, although the SYA is a statutory organisation. The position has not changed very much by the third stage. This is partly because the social workers do not have any problems about working with Frances without her parents' knowledge, and could consider helping her to leave home, at least temporarily, to go to a refuge, if they thought the situation required this. There is an increased likelihood of referral to a CDC or the SYA, but these formal measures are still based on voluntary co-operation.

At the final stage, all but one of the social workers felt that as voluntary co-operation had not been achieved, the children's safety required the use of judicial powers. This would in the first place mean referral to the mediation committee (see Chapter 4). As this can be done by any agency involved, the social workers all had direct access to this possibility. The social workers saw no difficulty in using statutory powers. They did not expect to need to make an emergency referral, although the possibility was mentioned. They expected to refer to the mediation committee, which would signal the strong possibility of legal action if the parents did not respond. The authority of the social workers seemed to rest on their confidence that conflict between themselves and the parents would be explored in a setting which would allow for the resolution of the conflict, but which would have authority if resolution was not possible. Whereas for the social workers in the Netherlands there was a chain of delegated authority leading to the judge for children, for the Flemish social workers there was an area in which authority was negotiated, and only when this failed would the legal authority of the judge become a factor. Confidence in the social workers' professional competence, on everyone's part, was fundamental to the negotiation of authority.

## Francophone Belgium

The social workers in the Francophone community of Belgium, have a system that is in many ways similar, although it replaces the mediation committee with a *conseiller*, who is part of the *Service d'Aide à la Jeunesse* (SAJ). Although at the first stage they expected to work without involving the legal powers of the state, they saw those powers as available, and available not only to themselves, but also to members of the family. They considered that the grandmother or the mother could invoke legal protection through an approach to the public procurator, and they would prefer the family to take this action rather than themselves. They expected to work on a voluntary basis and promote the ability of the family to protect itself. At the second stage, they were considering referral to the SAJ, but this would still keep the family in voluntary negotiation; like the Flemish SYA service, the SAJ only works on a voluntary basis. If the family was referred to the *conseiller*, he would have tried to negotiate a voluntary working agreement between the family and the social worker. If he had failed, he could have referred the case to the judge. Thus the social workers (whether in a voluntary organisation, a local social services office or the SAJ) have the possibility of getting help from a higher authority, the *conseiller*, in resolving a stuck situation, without having to resort to compulsory powers. Like the Flemish social workers, they have the possibility of negotiated authority. At the third stage, the social workers were clear that they would refer the family to the *conseiller*. They also considered that the school, one of the parents, the grandmother or Frances herself could have referred the case. They considered it to be a realistic possibility for Frances, with their support, to lodge a complaint against her step-father. There were many indications that the responsibility for action was seen as being widely located in the community and not only the responsibility of the social workers; others could readily invoke the legal process and could be expected to do so. They saw their role as providing a source of help and understanding for the family.

At the final stage, they were certain that they would refer the case to the *conseiller* unless they got immediate co-operation. They had no anxieties about their ability or right to do this. If the children were suffering, the parents would not be able to prevent state intervention by refusing to co-operate. The professionalism of the social workers was an important factor in their power, and it was that, rather than statutory power, that defined their position as agents of the state.

The two Belgian systems make the most thorough and institutionalised attempt of all the systems discussed to avoid referral to the judge for children. One result of this is that once the judge for children is involved, the social work task is taken on by a different agency, so that there is a greater separation than in other countries between voluntary and compulsory social work interventions. This is likely to be a factor in the relationship between parents and social workers at all stages of intervention.

## Scotland

The Scottish social workers could see no grounds at stage one, for intervening in the family without their consent. They were clear that they had a duty as representatives of the state to offer help on a voluntary basis, but that equally, this required the co-operation and engagement of the family. A number of them had in mind the availability of referral to the children's panel, and the option that the grandmother herself could make such a referral. By the second stage, the social workers felt that they had a clear mandate to make inquiries involving other agencies, and considered a referral to therapeutic services. The role of the social worker as agent of the state is seen in terms of offering help rather than making compulsory interventions or investigations. At stage three, however, the statutory duties of the social workers became more pressing. They were very aware that they might need to initiate child protection procedures or intervention by the children's panel, and that there was a potential conflict between this and their need to build a trusting relationship with Frances. Their professional role was to continue to offer a protective and supportive relationship to Frances, while fulfilling their duty as statutory agents, and this might put them in a conflictual situation. Emergency legal intervention was a possibility, but a great deal depends on the information from Frances and the response of her parents. Unless Frances provided more information, legal action was not possible; if her parents respond to the social workers, legal action might be avoidable.

At the final stage, Frances' ambivalence, and the reluctance of her mother to seek help for Andrew, led many of the workers to recommend a referral to the reporter, but because there was so little contact with the family there was uncertainty whether the grounds for this could be made out. The social workers saw a clear need for intervention, but were uncertain whether a referral would be successful. However, the role of the children's panel with respect to child welfare appeared to make compulsory intervention possible, even though the adults were unco-operative and hard evidence difficult to come by. The social workers as agents of the state with respect to child welfare appeared to remain relatively empowered despite the impediments.

## England

As we recruited a new group of English social workers for each country studied (a few workers took part in more than one group), we have a wider basis for the responses of the English social workers. There were more similarities than differences in their responses, and we have globalised the results for the purpose of this discussion. The major differences were between the groups involved in the original French project, which met in 1991 before the Children Act 1989 was implemented, and the others, which met in 1994-5. In terms of the amount of time given to discussion of different aspects of the case, the primary concern of the early groups was evidence; the primary concern of the later groups was procedures.

The English social workers were from the outset very aware of their duty to the state, in particular the duty to investigate. For many of them, their first concern was to decide whether there was a child protection issue. If there was, this would legitimise their inquiries to other agencies. There was a conflict for them over their role as investigator and the rights of the parents to know what was happening. They wanted their investigative work to be done on a voluntary basis, but the relationship with the family was based on information gathering. Until this had been done, they could not tell whether they had a right to offer help; were these children 'in need'? In all groups, the workers located the problem within a procedural and a legal structure. At the second stage, the social workers were frustrated by the family's continued non-co-operation. They could keep in touch with the playgroup staff and others, but they felt that there was no way of monitoring the family effectively, given Andrew's poor attendance at the playgroup. The concern with monitoring, information, evidence, risk and possible procedural steps reflected their anxiety about the need to protect the children, but they were dependent on being able to establish contact with at least one of the parents to be able to do anything. If the children were likely to be at risk the social workers would have to act; but they could not discover whether they were likely to be at risk without information from the parents. This put the parents in a strong position as there was insufficient external evidence of abuse or neglect. The social workers were clearly the agents of the state, but the relationship between the parents and the state gave the parents considerable control of the situation. The need for the state to produce evidence to put before the law, give the parents blocking power if they chose to withhold information. By the time Frances had run away and returned home again, the social workers were referring to a wide range of possible statutory provisions, but always with the proviso that they needed more information. The parents had power to control the situation by withholding information. Frances too was in a powerful position, and this created a dilemma for the social workers. On the one hand they wished to work therapeutically with a 13 year old girl in distress. On the other hand, they wanted to get the evidence that would enable them to protect her and her brother; but if they got this evidence they could no longer maintain confidentiality. There was much discussion of the use of child protection procedures, but although there was the will to use the procedures to support work with the family, there were obstacles to doing this. One obstacle was the lack of evidence, another was the nature of the proceedings, which were seen as exceedingly difficult for the family and potentially damaging to future working relationships. There was not a consensus as to whether a child protection conference would be called at this point, although a large proportion thought that it should be. The situation was frustrating for the social workers. There seemed to be agreement about what was and was not possible for them in using the law, and they could see no clear way forward, either legally or procedurally.

At the final stage, when the family continued to keep the social workers at arm's length, the social workers felt more disabled than at stage three. Without evidence they were still unable to act to resolve the situation, but they felt increasingly that there was a need to act. There was a feeling that they had missed an opportunity at stage three, and yet at that point they were still unsure about their grounds for legal action. Their duty to protect the children was in conflict with the need to provide evidence. In this situation they could only continue to try to involve the family and adhere to procedures. They discounted the possibility of using the child assessment order. They could not find a way to reach the children to protect them while all the family members stayed silent.

The dilemma for the English social workers was that as agents of the state they had to:

- provide evidence for the state to put before the law in order to protect children;
- respect the autonomy of families and the rights of parents; and
- provide help and support for families where children are 'in need'.

The responses of the English social workers to the case scenario demonstrated the potential conflict between the first two of these duties, and the difficulty in holding on to the third, when caught up in this conflict. There were considerable differences between the different countries' groups of social workers in the emotional tone of the discussion. After several repeated experiences, we felt that we could not discount the characteristic reaction of the English social workers, not shared by any of the foreign groups, of frustration and anxiety. Frustration because they could not act, and anxiety because they should act.

## The location of power

These summaries build up a picture of the different experiences of social workers in different countries in trying to use the system they have for the protection of children. Where, for different systems, did the power lie? How did this change or develop during the course of the case? How did the social workers see their power and how comfortable were they with this?

## The place of the legal system

It is apparent that in detail all the systems function very differently, but the continental systems share certain similarities. The location of power was ultimately with the legal system, but the separation between the legal system and the state in England made for tensions in the English social workers' experience that did not occur elsewhere. This is not just a question of the level of importance attached to parental rights. In Italy, the social workers felt that they had little right to intervene in families unless asked by the family, but when they felt it was necessary for the protection of the children, they had no difficulty in calling on the power of the law, at first informally and then formally. The English social workers who shared some of the Italian workers' difficulties over intervention (for example, both groups felt that they could not interview Andrew without his mother's agreement), continued to be held up by the family's lack of engagement, and could not access the power of the law. Both groups of Belgian social workers represented systems where the most strenuous efforts were made to *avoid* recourse to the law, but *access* to the law was not difficult. The negotiating zones provided by the mediation committee and the *conseiller* were easy for social workers, family members and other agencies to access, and created a clear and straightforward route into the legal system while at the same time providing an alternative. The Scottish children's panel, although more closely integrated with the legal system, fulfilled a similar function. In the English system, social workers represented the state, and the state and the family were both equal before the law. In the continental systems, the welfare function of the children's judge blurs the distinction between the law and the state. This increases the accessibility of the law for social workers as agents of the state, and increases the authority of the social worker, who is invested with delegated authority from the judge. Thus the French, German and Dutch social workers could operate with considerable professional authority, able to use the power of the legal system in relation to parents. Another factor in this power relationship was the duty of the judge in all the continental countries, to hold a case permanently under regular review. The judge is faced with the failure (or success) of his or her judicial decisions, and this continuing involvement (usually, if not always, by the same actual person) locates long-term responsibility with the judge.

Social workers in England (and to some extent in Scotland) seemed to be both more and less powerful than continental social workers. In some respects, English social workers have a great deal more power than others. They have a great deal more power after a court order is made, because there is no automatic judicial review; all the continental social workers were amazed at the lack of any continuing involvement of the law. At the same time, before an order was made, the English social workers had less power because they did not have the same level of professional authority accorded to them and they did not have the delegated authority of the judge which made supervision orders a favoured option in other countries. The continental social workers saw the separation of the English social workers from the judge for children as at once giving social workers too much power in some areas of work and too little support in others.

## The child assessment order

An interesting anomaly in the English responses, was the attitude of the English social workers to child assessment orders (CAO). These were mentioned as an option by a number of English social workers, but always dismissed. They were sometimes dismissed as requiring evidence that was not available, and therefore not a possibility. They were sometimes dismissed as not being useful. The reasons given why they were not useful were either that they were too short to allow an assessment to be made or that Andrew (and the order was usually suggested in relation to him) was not old enough to explain what was happening to him and give any information. This resistance to using the CAO was striking. It was for just this kind of situation that the order was put into the Children Act. A text book on the Children Act comments: "if the authority has some indication of harm to the child, but is doubtful as to the proper course of action...an application for a child assessment order may be preferable (to an interim care order or supervision order)". (White *et al.*, 1990 p.100). That comment seems to describe the situation in our hypothetical case. The ADSS originally resisted the order on the grounds that: "the CAO would confuse staff and there would be a tendency to apply for the 'lesser order' putting the child 'at risk'." (Parton, 1991, p.180). These were not the problems for our social workers. Their resistance to using the order seems to stem partly from an unwillingness to use an order of which they had little experience. How would it work out in practice? And partly from a rather pessimistic view of what assessment could be made in a seven day period. Whatever the reasons for not wanting to use the order, the effect was to deny themselves one obvious way of compelling the parents to enter into some negotiations with them, short of full legal intervention. This neglect of one potentially useful resource made available by the Children Act 1989, demonstrates that the statutes are only one factor in a complex web of influences that determine the ways in which social workers carry out their task. What the law enables, other factors may disallow.

## Power in the English system

Is this unwillingness to use a coercive power an indication of the insecurity of English social workers in their role as representatives of the state? It would not be surprising to find that English social workers did feel insecure in this role. They have been attacked by the media, criticised by child abuse inquiries and increasingly fenced in by procedures and guidelines which imply that they are incapable of acting effectively on the basis of their professional judgement. Lawyers undermine them in court and the intervention of the guardian ad litem can feel like one more hostile intrusion into their attempts to do the best they can for the children and families with whom they are concerned. Compared with continental and Scottish social workers, English social workers seemed to be uncertain about their power and their professional standing. In this situation, procedures were as much a protection as a constraint. It is striking that the only worker who wholeheartedly endorsed the English system was from southern Italy; this worker did not have the support of the law, and lacked authority as a representative of the state. She described the family as almost inviolable by the state. She too would have welcomed procedures as a support and a legitimation of her role.

In her consideration of value positions in child protection, Fox Harding points out that:

"popular concern about child welfare is balanced by a perhaps equally strong concern…about the dangers of the state having excessive powers and making unwarranted intrusions into the privacy of domestic life. The family may be seen as some kind of 'bastion' against the power of the state." (Fox Harding, 1991, p.5).

It is still felt that the Englishman's home should be his castle. No more than any other professionals are English social workers insulated from the culture that they live in. Uncertain professional confidence is likely to be only one aspect of the reluctance of social workers to use their power to intervene in families. The reactions of English social workers will be located with the framework of English culture of which they are a part. The rights-based philosophy of Hobbes, which we have elsewhere (Cooper *et al.*, 1995) contrasted with the continental political philosophy derived from Rousseau, is dominant, and the need to defend the individual and by extention, the parents of a family, against the intrusion of the state, is strongly felt. In being unwilling to use the CAO, English social workers may be demonstrating a more general unwillingness to use power. They have a shared cultural concern that the state's powers are intrusive and should be sparingly used. Intervention is easily seen as destructive; in the words of one participant "we can't just go around breaking up families".

## Making changes

In none of the countries studied did the equation of power and responsibility work out identically; in none was the nature of relationships between social workers, the law and parents the same. There were differences and there were similarities, but the individuality of each system was striking. Child protection systems seem both to express and to demonstrate fundamental aspects of a country's culture and political philosophy. Child protection systems are therefore likely to be constantly changing and any but the most carefully constructed changes may have unpredictable and unintended consequences.

# Section Four:
# How new perspectives
# can help in England

This section is a single chapter in which we summarise the messages that we have drawn from this research and look for ways in which the perspectives from other countries can help us in redrawing the patterns of the English system.

# Chapter 10:
# Messages from Europe:
# conclusions

In this chapter we consider some of the messages from other European countries, and look at three areas where we see the possibility of change in this country. The *continuum* of child welfare, the need for *space* within the continuum and the social *context* of the continuum are described and then discussed in relation to the need for change in the English system. We then consider the structural, cultural and ideological factors that are likely to determine the possibilities for making changes, and affect the outcomes of change.

## Messages from Europe: alternative visions revisited

For English practitioners, managers and policy makers, there are many ways of understanding and reacting to the material presented in the preceding chapters. The list of messages that we offer below is not definitive or exclusive. However, our research suggests to us that elsewhere in Europe, in countries with similar socio-economic circumstances, viable child protection systems exist in which:

- the suffering of the child rather than the identification of abuse is seen as central. Children can, if it is considered to be in their interest, be interviewed without their parents' knowledge;
- children can decide, up to a much further point than here, not to have action taken;
- social workers can risk holding a situation so that a child has time to agree to intervention;
- social workers are recognised both by parents and other professionals as having authority;

179

- co-operation and co-ordination between agencies can happen without formal procedures;
- children can be protected without a register;
- social workers do not need procedures to cope with the inherent anxieties of the work;
- voluntary organisations are structured into the system and seen as an integral part of the overall provision of service;
- invoking the law to protect a child is seen as the responsibility of others as well as social workers;
- the law can function in the discourse of welfare;
- working in partnership takes place with less emphasis on parental rights; and
- working in partnership is facilitated by the social worker having confidence in their authority.

Not all these factors are present with equal force in all the systems that we studied, but in all except the English system they exist. They create the following possibilities.

## A flexible continuum

It is possible to have a system which allows for a flexible continuum between support and protection. This is achieved by an open door policy to families seeking help, where they do not have to be defined as 'in need', together with a legal system that has a flexible relationship with welfare and the welfare discourse.

## An intermediate space

An important aspect of such systems is the possibility of an intermediate space, sometimes represented by an institution and sometimes by a person-in-role, which allows for negotiation, dialogue and deliberation before the law becomes involved, and even when the law is involved. Wherever there is the potential for compulsion, there is bound to be a pre-legal arena in which the possibility or threat of compulsion creates a space for action which is not fully voluntary, which we have called semi-compulsion. Since the vast majority of cases involving suspicion of child abuse, or actual risk to children, do not come before the courts, it is important to give concentrated attention to how this space is defined and constructed. It represents a theatre in which large numbers of children and families find themselves as actors, and in which the wider society is a permanent audience. What kind of drama is played out there has been one of the main subjects of this book. Purely 'voluntary' partnership work between professionals and families shades into semi-compulsion in complex and subtle ways, and we would suggest that there is no absolute method of distinguishing between the two. However the conduct of cases in this 'grey area' may be crucially shaped by the nature of what happens at its boundary. In England the child protection conference is on this boundary, and we have suggested that alternatives, located at a similar point in the system, can set a very different tone for what takes place before this boundary is touched or crossed. The kind of authority which is invested in, and discharged by, these intermediate institutions legitimates the kind of authority carried by professionals in the rest of the non-compulsory sphere. Administrative and procedural institutions put a very different stamp on the character of practice than do negotiative, dialogic, and confrontative ones.

## Wider social responsibility for protecting children

In the systems that we studied, the flexible continuum and the intermediate space are supported by much greater involvement of the community as a whole in child welfare. It is possible to widen the responsibilities of agencies and individuals in relation to child protection. This happens when the social services department is not the only point of access to legal intervention, which, apart from emergency police powers, is the case here. In particular, the access of family members including children to the law is easier elsewhere. Accessibility increases responsibility and ownership of the system. In particular, the access of family members including children and young people to the law, and to intermediate institutions like the mediation committee, *inspecteur*, or *conseiller*, is central to the way most European systems function. Children and families have direct and usually informal access to people with decision-making power. The fact that other professionals and citizens in general can and do refer cases into these systems, means that responsibility for and ownership of child protection concerns is socialised, rather than being confined to professionals or administrators.

Another aspect of this widening of the community involvement in child welfare is the inclusion of voluntary agencies and local interest groups in children's services plans (by whatever name they are known in different countries). This is less social services dominated, for example in Germany, where the community basis of this planning is institutionalised at several levels of government.

We would like to consider in more detail these three potential attributes of child protection systems, which are common else-

where and which may be useful to us in England. What would be
the implication for such developments in England?

## The future of English child protection

### Creating a flexible continuum

For the last few years, since the publication of the Audit
Commission report (1994), there has been growing concern over
the need to increase support for families and shift the focus of
work from a preoccupation with child protection and investigation. This has proved to be difficult. There have been changes,
interesting experiments in some areas, a decline in the number of
cases conferenced and the numbers of children registered; but it is
not clear how far this has led to any actual increase in family
support.

From the point of view of the families who may be looking for
help, there are a number of barriers to getting support. A
comparative study of the experiences of parents with child welfare
interventions (Baistow et al., 1996) demonstrates how much more
difficult it is for English parents than French parents to tap into the
system, and further work in progress looks likely to confirm this in
relation to Germany. Some of the problems relate to organisation.
English parents were much more likely than French parents to
have to tell their story many times to different workers, and
'getting a social worker' was hard to achieve. More fundamentally,
English parents had to prove that their child was 'in need',
whereas French and German parents made their approach on the
basis that they wanted help.

The English preoccupation with criteria and thresholds is
essentially about keeping people out of a service system with the
implication that the system is malign; it is better not to be
involved. Our research so far does not suggest that in general
services in the English system are worse than in others; strengths
and weaknesses may characteristically be in different areas of
work, but over all, social workers and social work systems in
England work to the same standards as in other countries. In
England we appear to make great efforts to discourage intervention, yet shortages in service provision do not provide a full
explanation for this. Thresholds, at the same time as being a
means of selection, are a manifestation of an individualistic
philosophy that it is better not to need help and that needing help
is both a demonstration of weakness and likely to make you
weaker. Thresholds as a means of selection are also an expression
of a wish to be fair. If resources are short, it is fair to ration them,
and rationing requires not just a knowledge of what someone says

they need, but a measurement of that need against other people's needs. Thus the defence of thresholds is that, as well as discouraging dependency, they ensure that those most in need have priority in the distribution of resources.

The readiness of other child welfare systems to respond to requests for help without being overwhelmed by competing needs cannot be attributed to the existence of better resourced services elsewhere. There may be better resources in some countries in some respects, but not on a scale that would eliminate problems of choice. The difference is in the attitude of the child welfare institutions to the seeking of help. Parents may not always get the help that they want; but their *request* for help is regarded as legitimate, and something which should get a response. (This is reflected in the common use of the word 'help' in the titles of services, institutions and legislation). There is all the difference between being told "we can't give you the help that you want, but we will try to think of something else" and being told "you do not qualify for help".

The first threshold for English parents is proving that their child is 'in need'. The second may be to prove that their child is 'at risk'. It is well known to parents as well as social workers (and whether it is *true* or not is less important) that you can get resources, in particular that you can get an allocated social worker, if your child is on the register. This creates a double bind. "You must be a good parent. I will give you help to be a good parent but only if you first demonstrate to me that you are a bad parent. If you are a bad parent I may take your child away."

Reflecting on our experience of other European systems has led us to see the concept of 'thresholds' as essentially conservative. The idea operates to *preserve* the system as it is, but alters the criteria according to which the same interventions are triggered. It is the equivalent of adjusting the size of the 'mesh' in the fishing nets of the system, so that more or less different kinds of fish are caught at different defined points. But this assumes a basically linear conception of the nature of interventions and the development of cases which come to be defined as 'child protection'. At least two vital elements in any proper conception of the practice task are marginalised in this way of looking at things:

- if 'needs' and 'risks', 'support' and 'protection', are brought into a *relationship* with one another, then any particular case must be seen as a *configuration*, rather than as a balance sheet with a bottom line which indicates its position on a scale of threshold criteria. 'Risk factors' are in a complex interplay with

'protection factors', and one of the most vital of these centres
around the capacity for change;
- any assessment of risks *or* needs must then focus on the capacity
  of the parents, the children, or the entire family, to accept help
  and show potential (or the lack of it) for change or development. The purposeful activity of professionals, working in
  partnership with families, is thus a central determining factor in
  making an assessment — has intervention shown signs of
  working, including working to reduce risks, or not? The activity
  of the worker, and the responsiveness of the recipients, enters
  the configuration and becomes itself an object of assessment,
  even as it is the medium through which assessment is undertaken.

What we saw in other systems was a readiness to work with the
situation as presented, not, indeed, taking the views of the family
members as the only possible ones, but prepared to start from that
point, and to respond flexibly to the development of the situation.
This did not mean an abandonment of authority, rather the
reverse. It did involve a readiness to 'give time to time', if
necessary, to say 'no' to requests without the external support of
unmet criteria, and if necessary to use professional authority to
confront inadequate parenting.

A further reason for the discontinuity in the English system
seemed to us to stem from the 'heaviness' of the English legal
system. This was discussed elsewhere in more detail in relation to
France (Cooper *et al.*, 1995), but the position is similar in relation
to all the other systems that we studied. The process of the law in
England is formal and intimidating, and the degree of power that
social workers have after legal intervention, is far greater in
England than elsewhere (except perhaps Scotland). Parents and
social workers may have different agendas in wishing to avoid
engagement with the law, but social workers as well as parents fear
the process of the law and fear the power that social workers can
wield when an order has been made. If our system legitimated a
greater exercise of authority by professionals in the 'non-
compulsory' sphere, then we would 'take on' more situations
without the fear that this would lead to undue 'control' or an
infringement of 'rights'.

Giving time to interventions involving abuse or risk implies that
professionals feel supported in working with risk-laden situations
without resort to the courts or excessive proceduralism. Using
professional authority with families in pursuit of change to reduce
risk and make their predicaments more manageable implies

equally that professionals feel they have social and managerial backing for the use of such authority. Creating a continuum of family support and child protection depends heavily on a change of professional culture, supported by revisions to the structures and institutions which are the context in which all practice occurs.

### Creating intermediate space

A flexible continuum needs a space which is outside the legal framework but acknowledges that the authority of the law spills over into areas where it is not directly invoked. The police use of cautioning would be an example of a similar use of the authority of the law. We think that this space exists elsewhere, though it is not necessarily used in the same way in all countries. The mediation committee and the *conseiller* use this space to avoid the use of the law. The *inspecteur* and the judge for children use it to work with the family partly within the legal framework. The informal consultation with the *giudice tutelare* in Italy is similar. The child protection conference does not have the power to decide whether a case is taken to court, and thus operates in parallel to the law; there is no structural relationship between them. Here the administrative system is not the gateway to the law. Paradoxically, the fact that the child protection conference and the legal process are *not* integrated, does not in any way diminish the legalism of the process of the child protection conference.

A space is also needed within the law, where the authority of the judge is manifest, but where there is scope for negotiation over the range of the use of this authority. This is the area that is covered in other countries largely by an extensive use of supervision orders, and to some extent by a more flexible range of orders (or judicial actions) which can allow for more negotiation with parents over specific aspects of an order. In this space, the social worker is directly representing the authority of the judge, yet at the same time, in working with the family, can support parental authority. A great deal of work with families is done in this area, e.g. by the guardians in the Netherlands, and the social workers of the French AEMO teams. This is a very difficult area of work for English social workers. Supervision orders are much less frequently used here than in other countries, and social workers feel that they have very little power to make them work. The only authority the social worker has is the threat of care proceedings. This involves the social worker in making out a case which clearly identifies the parent as failing. There is no space for a reinforcement of official concern short of this, such as can be provided, for instance, in

France or Germany, by a meeting with the judge for children who can reinforce the seriousness of the situation but stop short of altering the legal basis of the work. The fact that parents and children may meet with a judge to discuss, remonstrate, complain and so on, within the context of a legal order being in force, both reflects and embodies a belief in the possibility of sustaining trust between families and professionals even where controls are operating.

Family group conferences and mediation services represent two examples of an effort within the English system to revitalise the centrality of trust and negotiation as the medium through which conflict is resolved, and acceptable plans are made for children at risk. In the context of children's services planning, we see no obstacle to the development of local initiatives which might enable the institutionalisation of such arrangements in a more far-reaching manner than anything hitherto attempted. Equally, there is no obstacle to government endorsing certain key principles which might inform local thinking, without thereby creating a constraining blueprint. One of the main purposes of this book is to show that in Europe as a whole, there is no single model for achieving this, and that particular national approaches are deeply embedded in history, culture and politics; some flow from more centralised and some from more devolved systems of government and accountability.

Creating these kinds of space is extremely complex. The most specific experiments we have studied have been the mediation committee and the children's panel. The mediation committee has not been working long enough for its functioning or its impact to be assessed. The children's panel has, and the way the system as a whole (the panels, the reporters and the social services departments) responds to the Children Act for Scotland will be enlightening; what changes will there be, and what potential changes will not take place?

### Widening social responsibility for protecting children

In Britain today, localism is back on the agenda. The question for child protection services is whether those with an influence over policy are able to grasp and articulate the potential of this revitalised agenda.

"Therefore the task for policy-makers who can take a long view is not so much to develop blueprints for a grand settlement, based on empirically fleshing out such theological ideas as 'subsidiarity', but rather to start from where we are and describe desirable and achievable strategies for long term change.

That starting point is a highly centralised system. Centralisation has been a long tradition in British public management." (Mulgan and 6, 1996).

We hope we have sufficiently impressed on readers that by bringing 'Messages from Europe', we are not attempting to introduce a new 'theology' into English child protection work. In Germany and other countries, subsidiarity is "empirically fleshed out"; it is an organic aspect of how services are structured, planned, and made accountable at local level, more a living faith than a theology. We would endorse the main point of the above citation — the need to start from where we are at in England in thinking about change — but we do hold that alternative models may be catalysts to creative thinking; the model is not one of enslavement, borrowing, or copying, but creative transposition, and this is nowhere more true than in the question of the relationship between social services and the wider citizenry. "Start from where the client is", in Perlman's famous phrase (Perlman, 1957), is a familiar concept to social workers, so 'starting from where we are', is an idea that may come more naturally to social workers than to politicians. As social workers, we can also make use of ideas from systemic family therapy about the value of reframing in promoting change. The different visions of child welfare that we are offered by continental and Scottish social workers can be a new element in the system, and reframe our problems in ways that may enlighten our understanding of them and make new solutions a possibility.

Some of the institutions and roles we have discussed in this book — the mediation committee, the children's panel — are constituted by other 'citizens' rather than professionals in role; some like the *inspecteur*, the *conseiller*, and children's judges in many countries, are professionals who maintain access in a meaningful way to the involved parties in child welfare cases and create a social space in which they are more joined to than separated from them as fellow citizens. *Power, access* and *social linkage* are the three elements which combine, in very different ways, to create the possibility of negotiative relationships at the nodal points in different child protection systems. We have discussed in Chapter 1 how we do not believe that the child protection conference does, or can, achieve the same ends.

The challenge for English policy-makers at local and national levels may then be to construct systems which embody four overlapping characteristics:

- the capacity to plan and co-ordinate services at local level in a manner which includes community representatives, and gives rise to services which properly reflect local conditions;
- the capacity to sustain the present benefits of a systematic approach to case planning and review alongside an approach which offers genuine 'space' to individual children, parents, and whole families to be *active contributors* to planning, decision-making, and negotiation, even in the most difficult and conflicted circumstances;
- the capacity to contribute to local social cohesion through investing child protection institutions with *social authority* in addressing the realms of both children and family's needs, and their protection. This entails an evolving engagement with questions of social norms with respect to child rearing, parenting, and risk; and
- the capacity to release professionals into doing their job in a sufficiently supported and protected, but still accountable, environment in which they are comfortable both as *agents of change and of moral authority*.

Needless to say, these four dimensions interlock and are mutually reinforcing, for better or worse.

## Making changes

In the discussion of 'difference' in Chapter 6, we looked at the highly complex interplay between *structure, culture, ideology* and *functioning*. How a system functions depends on the interplay between past and present structures, culture and ideologies; the functioning of a system will also itself influence structures, culture and ideologies. In attempting to make changes, these factors need to be taken into account.

### Structures — existing institutional frameworks of law and government

Many of the differences between English and continental practice can be traced back in part to the nature of the legal system in this country. Family courts having been fairly recently ruled out, it is unlikely that any change in legal structures will take place in the foreseeable future. Any changes to the child protection system would have to take account of the effect of adversarial law and be adjusted to defend itself against enslavement by the legal discourse.

The relationship between local government and central government is different in each country, but the division of social work tasks between the two does not emerge as an important determinant of social work practice. The different role of central government in other respects may be more important. The role of central government in issuing directives and guidance in this country is very much more pronounced than elsewhere (Scotland taking a midway position). The extent of central direction in England, through guidance and through financial constraint (rate-capping), has to be taken into account.

The relationship between government (central and local) and the voluntary organisations also differs. In the countries where the subsidiarity principle is important, voluntary organisations have a major part in service provision and play a far more important role in the planning of children' services. The basis of social work provision is a multiplicity of agencies, large and small, the state social services are then one element in the range of services. Where subsidiarity is less to the fore, in particular in France, the use of voluntary agencies to provide a social work service for the children's judge gives tham a very powerful position. As the use of voluntary and independent providers increases in the country, we are in a position of change already, and may be able to make use of this flexibility; but currently the financial dependency of our voluntary agencies increasingly constricts and subordinates their role.

### Cultures and values

Throughout the preceding chapters we have attempted to demonstrate the way in which child protection systems embody the value system of the community. Anything that runs directly counter to the values of the community is likely to be ignored or subverted. Thus in France, social workers have not used *adoption simple* as a means of achieving open adoption (Hetherington *et al.*, 1996). The adoption of older children does not fit with their idea of the family. Equally, as we hypothesised earlier, the child assessment order has not been used by English social workers to manage situations of parental non-co-operation because of anxieties about individual rights (see the quotation from the Lord Chancellor below). National culture and values are fundamental determinants of the functioning of systems; nevertheless, cultural values can and do change. Moreover culture can change as a result of structural change — the law can lead opinion. Culture is far from being a static factor in the equation.

However, some cultural values are established and persistent. Britain has long had the reputation on the continent of placing a high value on personal privacy and individual liberty. For Mozart, in eighteenth century Vienna, an English woman was a recognisable popular stereotype for freedom and independence — refusing to be 'pushed around' (*Die Entführung aus der Serail*). This is a stereotype which we probably feel happy to live with. A high valuation of individual freedom from government interference is reflected in many ways in our child protection system, and in the English participants' responses. One of the most frequent criticisms they made of the continental systems was that the concept of the state as responsible for and to families appeared paternalistic. However, cultural attitudes to rules, law, and authority in different countries form an extremely complex mix, combining in different ways in different places. In this particular web of values, a stereotype that the English like to have of themselves is that they respect law but are prepared to break rules. This implies a level of confidence in individual judgement. Child protection has a proliferation of rules, but other things have conspired to undermine the confidence, both of the public and of the social work profession, in the validity of their professional judgement. The Cleveland affair greatly increased the distrust of the public for social workers and, equally damaging, increased social workers' uncertainties about the legitimacy of their interventions in families.

It is unlikely that a deeply embedded national valuation of individual rights will change, and any structural change needs to take that into account. On the other hand, there may be ways in which the valuation of independent judgement which legitimates working without rules might be fostered. As it is, there are many rules, but recent cases have demonstrated that rules do not of themselves protect children, and may inhibit the use of understanding and initiative.

### Ideologies: professional and political

Ideologies at various different levels are involved in the shaping of the child protection system. **Professional** ideologies have, and have had, an important part to play in the shaping of child protection services. Professional ideologies are to some extent mediated by wider cultural values, but, as suggested by Lorenz (see Chapter 6), they are a significant and highly influential point of contact between social workers from different countries. The areas of disagreement between the English and the other social workers were not about professional ideology, but came at the points where professional ideology was expressed within particular and differing frameworks of value. Professional ideologies spring from various sources; the shared ideology of European social work may express in part shared aspects of European culture. It must also derive from a shared knowledge base and comparable practice experience. This enabled the social workers in all the countries we worked in to be very open to looking at other points of view, and very open to reframing their own experience. We saw no evidence that differences in professional ideology would create difficulties in adapting continental ideas to our own use; differences in political ideology are likely to be more significant. The currently fluid state of political ideology discussed in Chapters 1 and 2 may give us an unusual opportunity to effect change.

Parton (1991) gives a detailed account of the **political** ideologies (among other things) that went into the shaping of the Children Act 1989. The bill was not seen as 'party political' and the debates demonstrated a political philosophy rooted in a belief that state intervention is undesirable. For example, in relation to the child assessment order, the Lord Chancellor argued that:

> "The child assessment order would necessarily be a major interference in family life. One can make of it as little as one likes, but it is a compulsory intervention that is in question, and it would raise the unsettling prospect of further intervention." (*Hansard*, HoL, 16 February 1989, Col. 316, quoted in Parton, 1991 p.181).

The child protection system is also affected by the political philosophy which has generated the social care market. Although this was first put in place in relation to community care, the approach to the provision of services for children and families, is increasingly dominated by a distinction that turns social workers into managers of cases rather than case workers. This has a knock-on effect on the nature of the provision of services by voluntary agencies, who are now mainly providers. Thus at the same time as there is a thrust to develop more agencies within the child welfare services which are not run by local government (as noticed above), the control of these services is being more and more extensively 'managed' by local government.

## Turning the wheel of change

If, as was argued in Chapter 9, child protection systems demonstrate an aspect of the relationship of the state to the citizen, then the relationship of the English citizen to the state seems to be in some need of repair. At the most negative there can be seen a spiral of distrust, from parents to social workers, from social workers to managers, from local government to central government and back again. This is fostered by media attention which readily scapegoats social workers. But equally, looking on the positive side, there is active concern, incredibly hard work at all levels and widespread evidence of good social work practice and rigorous thinking. The attention paid to child abuse by all, from central government to field social worker, is impressive. That the media should also be attentive may be less welcome, but is likely to be part of the same process. We would suggest that this avid attention is because of a general feeling that all is *not* well. The English system seeks to channel two opposing currents, the freedom of the individual, and the protection of the powerless. The current of individual freedom battles with the current of protection. At the confluence are families and social workers, caught in a maelstrom where survival is the best that can be hoped for.

In the opening chapters we considered the position of child protection and the work of social workers in child protection, in relation to the place of 'the social' in England at this time. The most fundamental difference that we saw between English and continental systems was the lack in England of a social contract between the citizen and the state. This contract existed in some form in all the continental countries that we studied, and informed the whole process of the relationship between families and the state. Part of the contract between the citizen and the state concerned their mutual expectations of each other regarding families and the nurture of future citizens. With a basis in the constitution, and not only in particular laws, the parent and the state are both responsible for the child as a future citizen; this relationship rests on reciprocal rights and responsibilities which are binding on both sides. Chapter 9 looked at the way in which this relationship expressed itself in our research material, and demonstrated the effect that the lack of a social contract has on the ability of English social workers to deliver care and protection to children. The ability of our child protection system to change may be closely connected to much wider social changes over which we, as social workers, have little control, but where we, as social workers, have a particular understanding and perspective that we should make known.

However, there are areas where we can make a more direct contribution to change. We have described the directions in which we consider the English system needs to move in order to respond to the call from the Audit Commission, and we have outlined factors that need to be taken into consideration. Governments and managers can change structures, but the development of structures that are consonant with the culture of the community entails the commitment of the community. While there are aspects of change that require a lead from the top, change also needs to be accepted within the community, both nationally and locally, and within the social work profession.

In all the changes that we have suggested, changes of attitude and perspective need to accompany and sometimes lead other changes. It is here that social workers as individuals and collectively may be able to feel their effectiveness in creating a better deal for the children and families they work with. Turning from investigation to support requires a mental reframing of the problems to be worked with; the commitment to child-centred work within the social work profession is not in doubt. It is less clear to social workers how they can achieve it. If we — and not only social workers, but all the professions concerned — can get ourselves off the hook of identifying abuse and look instead at the suffering of the child, we may be able to respond more readily and effectively to the desperation of families in distress. Then we may be able to deconstruct and reconstruct our child protection system into a child welfare system that both supports and protects.

# Glossary

*AEMO Judiciare* (France). A judicial order on a child or children imposed by the children's judge usually for a period of one or two years, while the child remains at home. A judicial AEMO is broadly comparable to a supervision order in the English system.

*AEMO administrative* (France). A non-judicial order authorised by ASE, the specialist child care service of the local authority. It provides access to resources for children and families on the basis of an agreed intervention contracted between the family and the social worker.

*Area Child Protection Committee (ACPC)* (England). This committee comprises representatives from local authority social services departments, the police, the community health services, and education services. It is responsible for co-ordinating child protection practice in the area.

*ASE — Aide Sociale à l'Enfance* (France). The specialist children's social service within all local authorities, ASE is at the centre of the system of administrative protection for children.

*Assistante Maternelle* (France). A foster parent or childminder who cares for children on a day time basis.

*Assistant Social de Secteur* (France). A local authority social worker who will normally be a 'generalist' with responsibility for a small 'sector' of population.

*Assistente Sociale* (Italy). Social worker.

*Associations* (France). A general term for 'voluntary organisations' which are very widespread in France and much more influential politically in France than England.

*Audience* (France). A hearing with a family in the office (*cabinet*) of the children's judge. The atmosphere and setting of the hearing is informal, presided over by the judge, but without ceremony or robes. The family's social worker will usually be present, but rarely any lawyers.

*Child (Care and) Protection Board* (the Netherlands). The central government service for the investigation of child protection cases for the judge for children.

*Child Protection Conference* (England). A conference usually initiated and chaired by the social services department to consider cases where there is concern about the safety of a child. It is attended by representatives from the police, and other professionals who have knowledge of the family. Parents, and if appropriate, the child concerned are also able to attend. The conference can decide to place a child on the register of 'children at risk' (see below) and formulate plans for the future protection of the child. The conference appoints a 'key worker' to co-ordinate and monitor such plans.

*Child Protection Register* (England). A record that is kept of children who are deemed by the child protection conference to be 'at risk'. The purpose of the register is to alert all agencies who may be involved with the child of potential danger.

*Children's Hearing System* (Scotland). This was established in Scotland under the Social Work (Scotland) Act 1968, following the deliberations of the Kilbrandon Committee. The Hearing System involves no formal separation between child protection and juvenile crime cases, and once matters of fact and law have been established, if necessary by referral to the sheriff, concentrates on welfare aspects of the case ('needs' rather than 'deeds'). Cases in which compulsory measures of care are implemented are reviewed regularly. There is an acceptance that decision-making patterns will reflect local concerns and conditions. Although the system has widespread professional and public support in Scotland, there has been continuing uncertainty about the capacity of children's panels to manage the complex issues in some cases.

*Children's Panel* (Scotland). The body which conducts children's hearings in Scotland. The panel consists of three members, including one member of each sex, one of whom chairs. Panel members receive some training and continuing counselling. The panel can decide if the child is in need of compulsory measures of care, and about the contents of these measures. Panels co-operate intensively with social services departments. Each local authority has a Children's Panel Advisory Committee which is responsible for recruiting and training, and ensuring that panel duties are properly carried out.

*Children's Services Plan* (England). Local authorities in England and Wales are required to produce children's services plans in co-operation with other services involved with children in their area, particularly health and education. This requirement is new and few plans have yet been published.

*CISS — Circonscription d'Intervention Sanitaires et Sociales (France). A district of the local authority social services (DISS).* Each department is divided into a number of geographical areas *(circonscriptions)* of about 50,000 inhabitants, each of which is covered by a multi-disciplinary team. Each *circonscription* is divided into sectors covered by one *assistant social.* Thus a local authority generic social worker is often known as an *assistant social de secteur.* The system has some resemblence to 'patch' organisation in Britain.

*COAE — Consultation d'Orientation et d'Action Éducative* (France). A service of the DPJJ which works closely with the children's judge. A multi-disciplinary team which carries out observation orders and assessments in the community. The team will give an expert opinion to the judge before a long-term decision or order is made.

*Commission de Prévention* (France). A meeting of the CISS multi-disciplinary team attended by the *inspecteur* who must gain parental consent to the course of action proposed by the commission, unless it proposes referral to the children's judge.

*Conditions d'Éducation Gravement Compromisés* (France). 'Conditions of upbringing which are severely compromised' — the criteria which informs a decision to refer a child protection case to the children's judge. The condition does not have to be proved and the law of 1989 relative to the protection of children states that where a child is 'a victim of ill-treatment, or is presumed to be so, and it is impossible to assess the situation or the family manifestly refuse to accept the intervention of the ASE' the case should be referred to the judicial authority without delay.

*Confidential Doctor Centre* (Flanders). These centres are run by voluntary agencies such as *Kind in Nood.* They provide a confidential treatment service for families in relation to child abuse. They accept referrals from parents, children, other professionals and members of the public.

*Confidential Doctor Service* (the Netherlands). A service providing a confidential response to anyone wishing to refer a family in relation to suspected child abuse. The service offers confidentiality to family members and to people outside the family (whether professional or members of the public). The service does not usually offer treatment, but co-ordinates and makes available other services to help the child and family. It also collects statistics for the child care and protection board.

*Conseille de l'Administration d'Aide à la Jeunesse (CAJJ)* (Francophone Belgium). The government appointed body which runs the SAJ and the prevention services for children and young people.

*Conseiller* (Francophone Belgium). The director of the social work service of *Aide à la Jeunesse*. S/he has responsibility for referrals (via the office of the public procurator) to the judge for children. S/he has to meet all families who may need to be referred to the judge and attempt with them and their social worker to arrive at a voluntary plan. Parents and children as well as social workers can request a meeting with the conseiller.

*DISS/DASS — Direction d'Interventions Action Sanitaires et Sociales* (France). The social services department of the local authority.

*DPJJ — Direction de la Protection Judiciare et da la Jeunesse* (France). This is a state service with a local organisation in each *department*. Established in 1945 to work with juvenile delinquents, this is still its major role, but services like COAE are extensively involved in child protection assessment and short term work.

*Éducation* (France). One of the central concepts of French social work, it denotes something much broader than just teaching or learning, including the idea of the child's total social, emotional, and environmental development and well-being.

*Éducateur Spécialisé* (France). A social worker trained in the principle of *éducation* to work with children, young people and their families.

*Education Department* (England). A department of English local authorities responsible for pre-school, primary, secondary and further educational provision. Educational departments employ education welfare officers who work closely with schools.

*Erziehungskonferenz* (Germany). See *Helferkonferenz*.

*General Practitioner (GP)* (England). Community-based family doctor in England.

*Giudice Tutelare (GT)* (Italy). A judge attached to the Italian youth court, who has oversight of orders made by the court; can appoint 'guardians' who will be responsible for the care of a child, and is available for informal consultation with social workers or families.

*Government of Flanders Youth Assistance Act (1990)* (Flanders). The Act replaced previous legislation and wording by replacing the words 'youth protection' with youth assistance which increased children's rights and right of audience after the age of 14 and stresses locally-based voluntary services to facilitate change. If these fail mechanisms are in place to exert coercive pressure before the mediation committee (see below) refers a child or youngster to the court.

*Guardian* (the Netherlands). A person who is made responsible for the welfare of a child by the judge for children where the parents are failing to provide satisfactory care. Non-governmental organisations provide guardian services which are used by the courts. The guardian is then in effect the allocated social worker, and works closely with the judge for children. A child who is on a guardianship order may be living at home, or may be in a placement.

*Health Visitor* (England). A service of trained nurses who undertake visits to all families where there are children under five. They advise on health and child-rearing issues.

*Helferkonferenz, Erziehungskonferenz (Helpers' Conference or Meeting)* (Germany). A meeting of professionals similar to a strategy meeting which then usually leads to a helpers' planning meeting to which parents, children and other family members are invited.

*Inspecteur* (France). The central figure in the 'administrative' sphere of French child protection. Not necessarily social work trained, she or he is responsible for formal assessment processes with respect to families with children at risk, for deciding on the implementation of *AEMO administratives*, and for making referrals to the children's judge.

*Joint Child Protection Teams* (England). These comprise representatives from social services departments and the police, who review initial referrals of children who may be at risk, and determine the type of response that would be appropriate.

*Juge Pour Enfants* (France). Sometimes called the *juge d'enfants* or the *juge des enfants*, she or he is the central figure in the judicial sphere of the French child protection system. A *magistrat de jugement*, the judge is responsible for all cases involving juvenile delinquency or children at risk, and undertakes the same three year advanced training course as all other judges. The judge has a wide range of powers with respect to children who come before the court, but not the power to permanently separate a child from its parents.

*Jugendamt (Youth Office)* (Germany). The statutory youth service responsible for the delivery of comprehensive youth and social services to children, young people and their families at a regional and district level in conjunction with voluntary services whom they support and encourage in line with the principle of subsidiarity.

*Jugendhilfeausschuss (Youth Services Committee)* (Germany). A

committee at local and/or regional level consisting of representatives of the local community engaged with young people and
professionals who review existing need and provisions, and plan
for the future taking into account local conditions.

*Juvenile Justice team* (England). Section of a local authority social
services department specialising in work with young people who
commit offences. They prepare reports for court and supervise
community based court orders.

*Kind in Nood (Child in Need)* (Flanders). A confidential doctor
centre in Leuven — see Confidential Doctor Centre.

*Mediation Committee (sometimes referred to as 'Mediation Com-
mission')* (Flanders). The mediation committee acts as the last
reconciliation authority when voluntary aid threatens to fail and
strives to achieve a solution through acceptance of voluntary
help. The mediation committee consists of six members
appointed by the government of Flanders for a five year period.
Referrals to the committee can be made by parents, young
people, institutions, the special youth assistance bureau and
magistrates of the office of the public prosecutor responsible for
youth matters.

*Mesure* (France). A court order enforced by the children's judge.

*Pedagogie* (Continental Europe). The theory and practice of
guiding the process of children and young people's growth,
development and socialisation. Closely related to *éducation* as a
basic principle informing social work in France.

*Procuratore della Repubblica per i Minorenni* (Italy). A procurator
for minors who is responsible for promoting their judicial
recognition and the practical implementation of the rights of
minors. Upon receipt of a complaint that a child is in danger,
the procurator can order emergency action, refer the matter to
the youth court or instigate further enquiries.

*Protection Maternelle et Infantile (PMI)* (France). The public
health service for mothers-to-be and for parents with children
up to the age of six. They work preventatively but with special
responsibility for situations where a child is at risk. PMI
employs a range of medical and paramedical staff including
specialist community nurses for children (like health visitors).

*Regional Institute for Ambulatory Mental Health (RIAGG)* (the
Netherlands). A health service provision of out-patient care
which is an important resource in providing individual and
family-based treatment for children and young people.

*Reporter to the Children's Panel* (Scotland). The reporter is the
lynch-pin of the Scottish system, and receives all referrals to the
children's panel, and decides whether there are grounds for a

hearing. If not, the reporter's options are to refer back to the social services department for voluntary measures of care, to take no further action, or to arrange a hearing. Thus the reporter's role includes a diversionary element, central to the philosophy of the Scottish system. Reporters are drawn from a range of disciplines, although, law, social work and education predominate. Social workers, parents, children, or any member of the public may refer to the reporter, or seek consultation with him/her. Reporters provide legal advice to the children's hearing, but do not take part in proceedings.

*Safeguarder* (Scotland). Since 1985, a person appointed by the sheriff or the chair of the children's panel in cases where there is a conflict of interest between the child and the parents. Under the Children (Scotland) Act 1995, this must now be considered in every case, whether or not there is a conflict of interest.

*Service de l'Aide à la Jeunesse (SAJ)* (Francophone Belgium). The social work service of the Francophone community for work with children and families in difficulties.

*Service de Protection Judiciare* (Francophone Belgium). The social work service of the juvenile court, working with children and young people on judicial orders.

*Service Éducatif Auprès du Tribunal (SEAT)* (France). Each high court (*tribunal de grande instance*) has a *SEAT* service attached to undertake emergency investigations on the authority of the judge.

*Sheriff* (Scotland). The sheriff works primarily in the adult criminal justice system, but is called upon to determine whether children's hearings will proceed where there is conflict between the reporter and parents or others about establishing the grounds for a hearing. The sheriff is an experienced and qualified lawyer. He or she hears evidence in closed court from the reporter and parents. In the event of an appeal, the sheriff has the power to substitute his or her own decision for any made by the children's hearing.

*Social Services Department* (England). A department of an English local authority responsible for social work services for children, families, the mentally ill, physically handicapped and the elderly. Often there will be separate sections specialising in work with different client groups. Social workers employed by the department may be located in community-based teams, hospitals, or residential and day care settings. There is an increasing tendency for departments to 'contract out' many of their services to private or voluntary (not-for-profit) organisations.

*SOS Enfance* (Francophone Belgium). A non-governmental organisation which runs a confidential service for children and families where there are problems of child abuse. This is similar to the Confidential Doctor Centres of the Flemish community.

*Sozialpädagoge/Sozial Arbeiter — SP/SA (Social Pedagogue/ Social Worker — SP/SW)* (Germany). Both can be found in the statutory and voluntary sector and share similar educational and training pathways in courses of at least six semesters (three years) at an institution of higher education and a year of practical work in placement which is assessed as part of the professional qualification (diploma).

*Sozialpädagogische Familienhilfe — SPFH (Social Worker with specialist training in social pedagogy and family work)* (Germany). Specialists trained in intensive and long-term family support and teaching of parenting skills where families can no longer cope. This provision is now available by law as an alternative to the removal of children from the home or to facilitate their return.

*Special Youth Assistance Committees (SYA)* (Flanders). These exist in each administrative district and consist of government appointed members representative of youth organisations and services which take into account local ethnic and cultural variation. They can organise individual aid and initiate or maintain development for preventive measures along the principle of subsidiarity.

*Tribunale per i Minnorenni (TM)* (Italy). The youth court. This deals with both civil and criminal matters.

*Unità Sanitaria Locale (USL)* (Italy). Locally based, multidisciplinary health and social services teams.

*Vormundschaftsgericht (Guardianship Court)* (Germany). One of the courts which regulates parental responsibility for children and young people. The guardianship court deals with all matters pertaining to the welfare of children and young people and appoints guardians where parents are not able to meet parental responsibilities. Judges are trained and act as inquisitors as well as mediators.

*Youth Advisory Centres (JAC)* (the Netherlands). Services offering a confidential advice and counselling service for young people aged 12 to 25. They are run by voluntary organisations, and there is an almost (but not quite) universal availability of these services throughout the Netherlands. The centres work with the young person, and do not refer them to statutory services except with the young person's agreement.

# References

Audit Commission (1994) *Seen But Not Heard: Co-ordinating Community Child Health and Social Services for Children in Need*, London: HMSO.

Baistow, K., Hetherington, R., Spriggs A. & Yelloly, M. (1996) *Parents Speaking: Anglo-French Perceptions of Child Welfare Interventions?* London: Centre for Comparative Social Work Studies, Brunel University College.

Ball, C. (1996) 'The Children Act 1989 — Creating a Framework for Partnership Work with Families' in Morris, K. & Tunnard, J. (1996), pp.5-10.

Barzini, L. (1964) *The Italians*, London: Hamish Hamilton.

Batty, D. & Cullen, D. (1996) *Child Protection: the Therapeutic Option*, London: BAAF.

Bundesministerium für Frauen und Jugend (1994) *Kinder und Jugendhilfegesetz*, Bonn: 6. Auflage.

Burchell, G., Gordon, C. & Miller, P. (eds.) (1991) *The Foucault Effect. Studies in Governmentality*, London: Harvester Wheatsheaf.

Butler-Sloss, E. (1988) *Report of the Inquiry into Child Abuse in Cleveland 1987*, London: HMSO, CMND 412.

Castel, R. (1991) 'From Dangerousness to Risk' in Burchell, G. *et al.* pp.281-298.

Cooper, A., Freund, V., Grevot, A., Hetherington R. & Pitts, J. (1992) *The Social Work Role in Child Protection: An Anglo-French Comparison*, London: Centre for Comparative Social Work Studies, Brunel University College.

Cooper, A. (1994) 'In Care or En Famille?', *Social Work in Europe*, Vol 1. no. 1, pp.59-67.

Cooper, A. (1995), Review of: Anthony Giddens (1994), 'Beyond Left and Right: The Future of Radical Politics', *Social Work in Europe*, Vol. 2, no. 1, pp.62-65.

Cooper, A., Hetherington, R., Baistow, K., Pitts, J. & Spriggs, A. (1995) *Positive Child Protection: A View from Abroad*,

Lyme Regis: Russell House Publishing.

Cooper, A., Hetherington, R. & Katz, I. (1997) *Can Europe Show us a Third Way?*, London: NSPCC.

Cullen, D. (1986) 'Legal Notes', *Adoption and Fostering*, Vol. 10, no. 1, pp.52-53.

Dale, P., Davies, M., Morrison, T. & Waters, J. (1986) *Dangerous Families: Assessment and Treatment*, London: Tavistock.

Dartington Social Research Unit (1995) *Child Protection and Child Abuse: Messages from Research*, London: HMSO.

de Cauter, F. (1995) *The Commission of Mediation for Special Youth Assistance* (unpublished paper).

DOH (1991) *Working Together under the Children Act 1989*, London: HMSO.

Donzelot, J. (1980) *The Policing of Families: Welfare versus the State*. London: Hutchisons.

Downes, D. (1994) 'Serious Diversions: Juvenile Crime and Justice in Europe — Lessons for Britain', *Social Work in Europe*, Vol. 1. no. 2. pp.4-12.

Ely, P. & Stanley, C. (1990) *The French Alternative: Delinquency, Prevention and Child Protection in France*, London: NACRO.

Federal Law Gazette, no. 30 (1990), *Act for the Reform of the Law on Child and Youth Services* (Child and Youth Services Act).

Fox Harding, L. (1991) *Perspectives in Child Care Policy*, Harlow, Longman.

Garrapon, J. (1993) *Lecture*, Paris (unpublished).

Gibbons, J., Conroy, S. & Bell, C. (1995) *Operating the Child Protection System: A Study of Child Protection Practices in English Local Authorities*, London: HMSO.

Giddens, A. (1994) *Beyond Left and Right*, Cambridge: Polity.

Goldstein, J., Freud, A. & Solnit, A. J. (1970) *Beyond the best interests of the child*, London: Collier Macmillan.

Gray, J. (1996) *After Social Democracy*, London: Demos.

Hamill, H. (1996) *Family Group Conferences in Child Care Practice*, Norwich: University of East Anglia Monograph, 151.

Hetherington, R. & Sprangers, A. (1994) 'The Work of the Flemish Mediation Commission', *Social Work in Europe*, Vol. 1. no. 2, pp.50-54.

Hetherington, R. (1996) 'Prevention and *éducation* in work with children and families' in Batty, D. & Cullen, D. (1996) pp.95-110.

Hetherington, R., Cooper, A., Piquardt, R., Smith, P., Spriggs, A. & Wilford, G. (1996) *Eight European Child Protection Systems: A Preliminary Report*, London: Brunel University College.

Helm, S. (1996) 'A Country Brought Low by Horror', *The Independent*, 10.9.96.

Hill, M. & Aldgate, J. (1996) *Child Welfare Services: Developments in Law, Policy, Practice and Research*, London, Bristol and Pennsylvania: Jessica Kingsley Publishers.

Hirst, P. (1994) *Associative Democracy*, Cambridge: Polity.

Home Office & DOH (1992) *Memorandum of Good Practice on video interviews with child witnesses*, London: HMSO.

Hutton, W. (1996) *The State We're In*, London: Vintage.

King, M. & Piper, C. (1990) *How The Law Thinks About Children*, Aldershot: Gower.

King, M. & Trowell, J. (1992) *Children's Welfare and the Law*, London: Sage.

Kuhn, T. (1970) *The Structure of Scientific Revolutions*, Chicago: Chicago University Press.

Lebrun, M. (1992) *Horizons Jeunes*, Treignes: Service Intervention Recherche Jeunes.

Lindley, B. (1994) *On the Receiving End: Families' Experiences of the Children Act 1989*, London: Family Rights Group.

Lorenz, W. (1996) 'ECSPRESS, The Thematic Network in the Social Professions', *Social Work in Europe*, Vol. 3 no. 3, pp.25-29.

Marneffe, C. (1992) 'The Confidential Doctor Centre — A New Approach to Child Protection Work', *Adoption & Fostering*, Vol. 16. no. 4, pp.23-28.

Marsh, P. and Fisher, M. (1992) *Good Intentions: Developing Partnership in Social Services*, Joseph Rowntree Foundation and Community Care.

Ministry of the Flemish Community (1995) *Special Youth Assistance in Flanders*, Family and Social Services Administration Special Youth Assistance Section.

Ministerie van Justitie (1992) *Family Supervision Orders*, the Hague: Ministerie van Justitie.

Ministerie van Justitie (1993) *Child Care and Protection Boards*, the Hague: Ministerie van Justitie.

Minozzi, M. & Tomassi, R. (1994) 'Telefono Azzuro: Italy's Child Helpline', *Social Work in Europe*. Vol. 1. no. 1.

Morris, K. & Tunnard, J. (Eds) (1996) *Family Group Conferences: Message from UK and Research*, London: Family Rights Group.

Mulgan, G. & 6, P. (1996) 'The local's coming home: decentralisation by degrees', *Demos Quarterly*, 9, pp.3-7.

Neate, P. (1991) 'A Different Way of Working', *Community Care*, 10.10.91.

Parton, N. (1991) *Governing the Family; Child Care, Child Protection and the State*, London: Macmillan.

Parton, N. (1996) 'Child Protection, Family Support and Social Work', *Child & Family Social Work*, Vol. 1, no. 1, pp.3-11.

Perlman, H. (1957) *Social Casework: a Problem Solving Process*, Chicago: University of Chicago Press.

Pieck, A. (undated) *Special Youth Assistance in Flanders*, Ministry of the Flemish Community.

Pitts, J. (1995) 'The Relationship Between Social Work and the Law in the Juvenile Justice and Child Protection Systems of England and Wales', in *Droits et Societe*, Paris: Ministry of Justice.

Pogge von Strandmann, H. (1994) 'The New Social Work in East Germany', *Social Work in Europe*, Vol. 1. no. 3. pp.4-9.

Ruxton, S. (1996) *Children in Europe*, London: NCH Action For Children.

Salgo, L. (1992) 'Child Protection in Germany', Ch. 20 in Freeman, M. & Veerman, P. (eds.), *The Ideologies of Children's Rights*, Netherlands: Kluwer Academic Publishers.

Saraceno, C. & Negri, N. (1994) 'The Changing Italian Welfare State', *Journal of European Social Policy*, 4 (1).

Santosuosso, A. (1991) *I Tuoi Diritti*, Milan: Hoepli.

Schäfer, H. (1995) 'The Principle of Subsidiarity: a New Magic Formula for the Construction of the European Community?', *Social Work in Europe*, Vol. 2. no. 3. pp.52-3.

Soydan, H. & Stal, R. (1994) 'How to Use the Vignette Technique in Cross-cultural Research', *Scandinavian Journal of Social Work*, Vol. 3. pp.75-80.

Thoburn, J., Lewis, A. & Shemmings, D. (1995) *Paternalism or Partnership? Family Involvement in the Child Protection Process*, London: HMSO.

Trowell, J. (1996) Private communication.

Wells, H. G. (1986 edition) *The History of Mr Polly*, London: Longman.

White, R., Carr, P. & Lowe, N. (1990) *A Guide to the Children Act 1989*, London: Butterworths.

Zeldin, T. (1995) *An Intimate History of Humanity*, London: Minerva.

# Index

# POSITIVE CHILD PROTECTION
## A View from Abroad
By Andrew Cooper, John Pitts, Karen Baistow,
Rachael Hetherington, and Angela Spriggs

This important book *"enticed me to keep reading when I
should have been doing something else!"* **Adoption and
Fostering**. It draws its lessons from participative action-
research undertaken over three years with social workers,
children's judges, magistrates, health care professionals, and
children and families involved in social work protection cases
in England and France. It offers new insights into:
> - ways in which genuine partnerships between social
> workers and families, and between social work and the
> courts, can be achieved in child protection
> proceedings.
> - models of practice and supervision which will
> minimise social worker burn-out.

What *Positive Child Protection* shows is almost like a different
world, where social workers are secure from violence,
respected, trusted, even admired. *"Could we achieve it
here?...The book leaves a feeling that child protection can be
positive, welcomed and valued...Positive child protection
indeed."* **Community Care**

Paperback    184 pages    1-898924-35-X
Available from Russell House Publishing Ltd,
38 Silver Street, Lyme Regis, Dorset DT7 3HS